IDENTIFYING SUICIDE POTENTIAL

Social Problems Series
Sheldon R. Roen, Ph.D., Editor

IDENTIFYING SUICIDE POTENTIAL

Conference Proceedings, Teachers College, Columbia University,
New York, New York, December, 1969

EDITED AND WITH COMMENTARIES BY
DOROTHY B. ANDERSON and **LENORA J. McCLEAN**
Teachers College, Columbia University, New York, New York

BEHAVIORAL PUBLICATIONS, INC.
New York, New York

HV
6545
.C6
1969

Library of Congress Catalog Card Number 78-140045
Standard Book Number 87705-024-4
Copyright © 1971 by Behavioral Publications

Behavioral Publications, 2852 Broadway—Morningside Heights,
New York, New York 10025

Printed in the United States of America

Contents

Contributing Authors

Dorothy Bruhl Anderson, R.N., M.S., *Clinical Associate, Mental Health-Psychiatric Nursing, Graduate Program, Teachers College, Columbia University; Formerly Staff, National Save-A-Life League, New York, New York*

LeClair Bissell, M.D., *Coordinator, Alcoholism Service, Department of Medicine and Psychiatry, Roosevelt Hospital, New York, New York*

Carlton H. Blake, M.D., *(private practice), Assistant Director, Soundview, Throgs Neck Community Mental Health Center, Bronx, New York*

Karen Pfanku Blaker, R.N., M.S., *Instructor, Graduate Programs in Mental Health-Psychiatric Nursing, New York University; Consultant and Counselor, National Save-A-Life League, New York, New York*

Howard M. Bograd, Ph.D., *(private practice), Formerly Chief, Suicide Prevention, Queens Hospital Center, New York, New York*

E. Alden Ellison, M.D., *(private practice), Attending Psychiatrist, Roosevelt Hospital; Consultant, National Save-A-Life League, New York, New York*

M. Leah Gorman, R.N., A.M., Ed.D., *Director of Graduate Programs, Mental Health-Psychiatric Nursing, New York University; Formerly Instructor, Teachers College, Columbia University, New York, New York*

Cathleen Greene, M.S.W., *Cornell Program in Social Psychiatry, The New York Hospital, Cornell University Medical College, Ithaca, New York*

Ari Kiev, M.D., *Chief, Cornell Program in Social Psychiatry, Clinical Associate Professor of Psychiatry, Cornell University Medical College, Ithaca, New York*

Ronald Maris, Ph.D., *Associate Professor of Social Relations and Psychiatry (Sociology), Johns Hopkins University, Baltimore, Maryland*

Lenora J. McClean, R.N., M.A., *Clinical Associate, Mental Health-Psychiatric Nursing, Graduate Program, Teachers College, Columbia University; Consultant, National Save-A-Life League, New York, New York*

The Rev. Robert B. Reeves, Jr., S.T.M., *Chaplain, Columbia-Presbyterian Hospital Center; Clinical Associate in the Program in Psychiatry and Religion, Union Theological Seminary, New York, New York*

Joseph Richman, Ph.D., *Senior Psychologist and Assistant Professor, Bronx Municipal Hospital Center, Albert Einstein College of Medicine, Bronx, New York*

Acknowledgments

Much of the success of the Conference on Identifying Suicide Potential for which these papers were originally developed can be attributed to all those who lent their time, energy and talents to our endeavour. Particular appreciation goes to Elizabeth Maloney, our Project Director in Mental Health-Psychiatric Nursing, and our Department Chairman in Nursing Education, Elizabeth Stobo, for their wholehearted encouragement and support. Our colleagues, Mary Ramshorn, Leah Gorman, and John Gorton, were of invaluable help. Karen Blaker not only participated in the conference but generously shared her own experience in conference planning.

Others to whom we are indebted include conference participants and discussion leaders, our graduate students in the graduate program of Mental Health-Psychiatric Nursing, as well as our wonderful audience.

Mrs. Estella Lucas was a faithful and patient secretary without whom our best intentions would have remained unprinted. Finally, our appreciation goes to Mr. Harry Warren, President of the National Save-A-Life League, who has generously facilitated and encouraged our participation in suicide prevention.

Introduction

The astounding growth of suicide prevention resources in this country can be attributed largely to the numbers of concerned people who have boldly and generously responded to a problem which has baffled generations. Many of them began by working with suicidal individuals from their own homes or with small groups of interested friends and colleagues who shared the conviction that suicides can be prevented. Yet, while the success of suicide prevention can be endlessly documented, morgues across the country attest to the fact that suicide is being committed at least as frequently as it ever has been in America. The vast majority of these suicides are people whose destructive forces went unchallenged by any neutralizing or constructive efforts.

It was the commitment of courageous people in suicide prevention and the need to pool local resources to cope with the magnitude of the problem that inspired the two day conference in Identifying Suicide Potential at Teachers College last December. Participants from a wide variety of disciplines came as willing to share experience and responsibility as they were eager to learn from one another.

The focus of the conference was based on the obvious need to investigate and to learn how to recognize suicide potential in the population before people are in precipitous crisis or become grave statistics. Additionally, it was apparent that in order to multiply preventive efforts we had to spread our energies in many directions and across disciplinary lines in order to initiate some beginning coordination of effort which was sadly lacking in the New York area.

Participants in this conference brought divergent orientations and approaches to bear on a shared goal—that of affecting the high numbers of suicidal statistics. Many of the papers in this volume reflect the writers' concern about a particular aspect of suicidal phenomena or populations. Some papers are strictly essays, others are products of extensive research; many could have extended into volumes of data if time and space permitted and suggest areas for further research and exploration.

The involvement of all participants, audience and speakers alike, in each phase of the conference, including discussion periods following papers, contributed to the scope and profundity of the conference as a learning experience. We have attempted to convey this dimension to the reader through our editorial comments.

As the content for the conference was planned, we felt that attention needed to be drawn to some straightforward indications of the extent of suicidal phenomena in the population. The focus then moved to sociological factors relating to suicide and the interaction between suicidal individuals and social forces. The emphasis narrowed to the family system and special high-risk subgroups in society. The interaction of the so-called "gatekeepers," or those who might serve as a significant link between individuals, with small groups and other human resources was approached within the framework of Primary and Secondary Prevention.

The Appendix contains two edited documents by Ari Kiev and his associates for the purpose of educating the lay public to a more useful approach with relatives and friends of persons that are suicidal. Although not presented at the conference, these papers seemed a fitting example of what people in suicide prevention centers might use to help inform families and friends of clients. It is hoped that these additions will be seen as only one step in our obligation to involve the community at large in our efforts at suicide prevention.

Our experience with this conference confirms our belief in the power of human commitment to solve a distinctly human problem.

Dorothy Anderson
Lenora McClean

Part One

1: Suicide Prevention

Ari Kiev

In spite of the proliferation of suicide prevention services in the last ten years, the suicide rate in this country remains essentially unchanged. This raises some profound questions about the people and the problem: Who is suicidal? Where and how do suicidal people live? Further, what, if anything, are we preventing? How do we reach those who kill themselves, and how do we in related professions and lay workers learn to use ourselves more effectively?

The number of completed suicides in the United States each year is estimated at approximately 20,000 to 40,000 without counting indirect forms of self destruction resulting from auto accidents, industrial accidents, narcotic addiction and chronic alcoholism. It is the second most common cause of death in the college age population and the most common cause of death among young Negro women, and American Indian youths. To the extent that indirect forms of self destruction are particularly high among young people, the overall contribution of this age group to total deaths by self destructive acts is undoubtedly a larger part of the total than would be suggested by the reported rates.

Suicide risk is considerable in the elderly, the alcoholic, those with suicidal histories, and those with severe psychiatric disorders. The availability of lethal weapons, contact with others who have made

3

attempts, and recent major catastrophic stresses also increase suicide risk.

The magnitude of suicidal behavior is such as to constitute a major public health problem. Save for fluctuations during the Depression and world wars, the suicide rate has remained remarkably stable in this century. It has remained stable as the 12th most common cause of death since 1950.

The persistence of the same rate over time is particularly striking in view of the major advances in psychiatry which have occurred in the past fifteen years, especially the advent of the psychotropic drugs, the development of open-door hospitals and the resurgence of interest in community psychiatry. The resident mental hospital patient population has been reduced from 554,000 in 1954 to 363,200 in 1969, and is expected to be reduced still further by 1973 to 184,700. The number of psychiatrists has progressively increased from 2.6/100,000 population in 1945 to 11/100,000 in 1969 and there have been increases as well in the other professional groups actively concerned with the suicide problem. Despite the availability of potent antidepressant medications, a humanitarian approach to psychiatric disorder, and an increased number of people in the helping professions, the suicide rate has not changed significantly in the past fifteen years, nor is there any reason to assume that the rate of suicide attempts has declined.

There is an urgent need to examine what has been done and what must yet be done in the area of suicide prevention so as to make inroads on what appears to be an unchanging rate pattern.

SUICIDE PREVENTION CENTERS
FAIL TO MEET NEED

In the past fifteen years some 120 suicide prevention centers have been established throughout the country. Such centers have received considerable federal support and are to be an integral part of the community mental health centers now being developed. There is no evidence to date that any of these centers which in the main specialize in telephone referral, have reduced the suicide rate in the areas they covered. Some have found that only a small percentage, 15% in one report, of calls relate to suicide and that these are predominately low suicidal risks. There are some who suggest that these centers be called crisis intervention centers since few of them provide treatment.

Only 4% (7 of 158) of the suicide attempts we have studied in the past two years called a suicide prevention center number prior to their suicide attempt. Closer examination of the data suggests an explanation for this. The suicidal act in most of our patients was characterized by impulsivity and the absence of premeditation, even in the most dangerous attempts. Patients were often so emotionally disturbed at the time of the attempt that they not only did not consider but could not use the telephone to call for help. It is likely that those who kill themselves are similarly disturbed and cannot call for help at the moment of maximum suicidal drive. Another factor which cuts across age, sex and diagnostic groups, was non-recognition of an underlying psychiatric illness or emotional disturbance which the patient was experiencing prior to the attempt.

Although many of our patients had been troubled for considerable periods of time, 41% (64 of 158) were not in treatment prior to the attempt. Most did not feel that they were ill or that their symptoms required treatment. Most believed their symptoms would pass. Symptoms were usually rationalized in terms of life difficulties or the patient's personality. Thus, 34% attributed their symptoms and their suicidal attempt to interpersonal conflict; 8% attributed their difficulties to alcohol; 7% attributed their difficulties to drug abuse; and 6% attributed their difficulties to social isolation. Only 21% attributed their difficulties to what they considered a psychiatric illness.

It appears that the lowest risk patients are most likely to utilize the suicide prevention centers, and that the highest risk groups are least likely to be in touch with such centers. This may be due to characteristics of the patients. Passive dependent people are likely to think but not act suicidally and are likely to rely on the telephone to establish links with others while the individual most likely to act on his drives is also most likely to eschew seeking help. That those at greatest risk are least in touch with the kinds of prevention centers which have been most vigorously and most abundantly developed does not mean that such prevention centers have no place. They do most certainly serve an important function as crisis intervention centers. Other types of programs however must be developed to reach the highest risk groups.

Even when the net is widened to bring more suicidal risks into the medical network one must still contend with the specificity of current social and psychiatric treatments for specific patient groups. It is important to pay attention to the different patterns of suicidal behavior which respond differently to conventional forms of psychiatric treatment. In our own experience we have had considerable difficulty in preventing repeated attempts, some of which were dangerous in certain impulsive patients, irrespective of the approach used. However preliminary analysis of the data suggests that treatment may reduce the frequency of repetitive attempts and may also shorten the time required for psychological recovery from them. Many of these patients who make repeated attempts have been in touch with family physicians and/or psychiatrists and indeed in a fair percentage of cases have received adequate antidepressant therapy and psychotherapy. These facts suggest that such efforts may do little for impulsive immature patients who make repeated attempts.

RECOMMENDATIONS

We must develop new methods for widening the treatment net and delivering care to high risk groups which are not now being reached. We need better coordination among existing agencies, and new methods of treatment. I would like to make several concrete suggestions along these lines.

1. The suicide prevention centers receive most support at the present time. They must clarify their objectives, analyze their day to day operations, and determine whom they are helping. If the center decides that its major objective will be to prevent suicide it must actively seek out the high risk population by initiating contact with old age homes, city shelters, and alcohol rehabilitation centers. Door to door canvassing in anomic areas with high rates of single room occupancy living situations might also establish personal ties between center personnel and high risk individuals who might develop regular patterns of telephone contact which might have considerable preventive effect. General practitioners and psychiatrists might even be interested in referring appropriate patients to the center for regular telephone contacts which they themselves cannot provide. There are some people who like to talk on the phone; housebound people who are perhaps elderly, disabled, and even phobic, might be recruited as volunteers or paid as telephone workers. They offer an enormous manpower pool to draw upon for the development of such extended suicide prevention work by telephone. The addition of picture screens to the telephone will make contact by telephone more personal and should provide further stimulus to developing the use of telephone programs beyond their present use.

The same considerations apply if the centers are to concentrate on crisis intervention work, although in that instance they would be better plugged in to other sources of referral like for example the police emergency number 911, not just for potential suicides as is now the case with the Save-A-Life League, but for other kinds of life crises. According to a *New York Times* report (Nov. 28) the public dialed 911 4,844,750 times (17,000 times a day) for the first nine months of 1969. Non emergency calls accounted for 59%-62% of all calls. The availability of 911 has led to an increased public demand for police services. To the extent that many of these calls are not emergencies, appropriate ones might be referred to crisis intervention clinics.

2. There is an urgent need for the development of training programs in the early recognition of psychiatric disorders and the initial phases of crisis intervention for physicians, ministers, union counsellors, management consultants, and community mental health workers. Included should be others who in the course of their daily work come into contact with high suicidal risk individuals with treatable symptoms. These symptoms are often either masked by other complaints, explained away by reasonable explanations, or justified as understandable responses to stressful events.

Some 65% of our patients had been in touch with a physician or psychiatrist in the months prior to their attempted suicide. Similar figures have been reported for completed suicides as well. Physicians must learn to avoid the common inclination to prescribe minor tranquilizers for anxiety and tension, and barbiturates for insomnia when further inquiry might reveal a depressive syndrome which would respond better to antidepressant medicines.

An additional problem is the patient's inclination to feel extra guilty and hopeless if his symptoms persist while he is being treated, which is likely to happen if he is receiving the wrong medicine. The patient's problems may be compounded by others in helping positions who attribute the patient's symptoms to insufficient will power or lack of motivation failing to recognize apathy and lack of drive as symptoms of psychiatric illness and as such somewhat out of the patient's direct control. The same error is made by the indiscriminate use of sensitivity training for increasing motivation.

The suicide rate among men is considerably higher than among women and indeed other population sub-groups. Yet the attendance of men in psychiatric clinics and in psychiatric office practice is considerably lower than that of other groups. In our society men do not enter the sick role very readily. For this reason it is important that active links be established with industry to increase awareness among those in counselling positions of the early signs and symptoms of psychiatric illness and ways to prevent the development of more serious forms of disability. The same applies to other settings such as schools, prisons and self help groups where people are already involved in problem solving and have considerable contact with the same individuals over time.

3. Efforts to extend the activities of suicide prevention centers and to maximize the utilization of human resources already engaged in helping activities are more likely to succeed by coordinating existing programs. The computer makes it possible to coordinate programs by establishing case registers of high risk individuals, storing and updating treatment records, and reducing duplication of effort. The availability of a central data bank containing information about special facilities and treatment interests should reduce unnecessary duplication of services and provide better care for those in need. Case registers can facilitate follow-up programs. To the extent that patients remain at risk not for one year but perhaps over an extended number of years, it may make sense to establish a framework for periodic follow-ups rather than to use up treatment efforts in one shot.

Better coordination can lead also to more efficient use of teaching personnel. Combining the special interests and skills of different programs ought to provide a comprehensive approach to the problem of suicidal behavior. It also ought to reduce the need for each program to develop additional activities for rounding out its program at the expense of the areas of expertise. At Cornell our special interest has been in the development of a treatment approach for patients who have attempted suicide, the development of data collection and data analysis techniques, and the development of training programs in the early recognition of mental illness and in crisis intervention techniques. We are working closely with a number of emergency rooms, and a poison control center which are equipped

to handle the medical emergencies of suicide attempts. We have a
very close working relationship with the National Save-A-Life-League
and serve as a major treatment resource for them. Such collaboration
is mutually beneficial and is by far the best way for developments to
proceed, as opposed to the current trend for each program to develop
a full range of techniques.

We are working in close collaboration with Encounter, a self help
non-residential therapeutic community for pre-addicts many of whom
have histories of suicidal behavior and some of whom in the course
of treatment become suicidal. We evaluate all prospective candidates
to Encounter to screen out those who are too disturbed to cope with
the rigors of the group approach and are in need of other treatment.
We also serve as a treatment resource for those who can't cope with
the group. Here again coordination makes it possible to take on that
small part of the total treatment process that is needed to support
ongoing activities in other agencies. In this way more individuals can
receive comprehensive care, albeit at different facilities and each
program can improve upon the activity it does best without being
fragmented by taking on too great a diversity of programs.

Through such intermediary contact, it is possible to learn more
about high risk groups not ordinarily in contact with psychiatrists or
public agencies and to provide treatment back-up for such groups.

4. There is an urgent need to distinguish between the various forms
of suicidal behavior in terms of seriousness of intent, dangerousness
of the attempt, methods used, primary psychiatric disorder, willing-
ness to accept treatment and other crucial dimensions which
influence the degree of individual suicidal risk. This differentiation
has important implications for the development of specific treatment
methods for specific patient groups, and for the critical evaluation of
the efficacy of the most common forms of treatment. Computer
technology now makes it possible to answer some of these questions
by comparing the experience of different programs. Information
collecting procedures must be standardized to implement such
studies. There is an urgent need for standardization of questionnaires

which can be used by various facilities and analyzed by standardized programs. We are now developing a precoded comprehensive interview form, a computerized data bank and programs for analyzing incoming data. We have already established links with a community mental health center, a private hospital, a poison control program, and several clinics in other countries all of whom will utilize the same forms and the same programs for the analysis of the data allowing us the opportunity to make useful comparisons between facilities and between various techniques applied to matched groups of patients.

Our own experience has suggested that the conventional model of psychotherapy which emphasizes the patient's responsibility for his difficulties, tends to heighten guilt and a sense of hopelessness in suicide-prone patients. This is true even when they receive appropriate antidepressant medicine, as was the case in 45% (41 of 91) of the patients in treatment in the series of 158 patients we recently studied. Indeed, this has much in common with the lay inclination to put the patient into the deviant role since it attributes motivational designs, or manipulative origins to the patient's symptoms and, indeed, the suicide attempt itself. That analytically oriented psychotherapy may not be an appropriate model for suicidal patients is also suggested by the data. These show that 83% (10 of 12) of patients who made three or more previous attempts, and 63% (41 of 65) of patients with one or two previous attempts had had such treatment; and that in fact, 51% (42 of 81) first attempters were in such treatment within the year preceding their first attempt.

We utilize a medical model of symptoms or illness which minimizes the patient's responsibility for his symptoms, tends to neutralize the patient's sense of guilt and reduce his suicide potential. It also reduces the pressure on the doctor, by assigning responsibility for symptom reduction to the medicine. This allows him to be more optimistic and hope inducing, since the result does not depend on the "will power" of the defeated patient, nor on the doctor's special therapeutic skills.

This medical model which relies heavily on pharmacological

reduction of symptoms, can be readily adopted by general physicians, who are usually the first to be consulted for the physical concomitants of depression. The work of non-psychiatrists, i.e. mental health professionals, paraprofessionals and community caretakers, is facilitated by the distinction made between psychobiological and social factors. They can continue their social and interpersonal approaches at the same time that the patient receives appropriate medicine for symptom relief from the general practitioner or psychiatrist.

We must ask ourselves which techniques are best for the impulsive psychopath, the isolated schizophrenic, the intractable depressive, and the disguised alcoholic, who account for large numbers of suicides, and are recalcitrant to treatment or unwilling to utilize prevention agencies.

Therapeutic social clubs and patient led groups must be developed and tested in specific groups of patients. We find in our own clinic that much of our staff time is taken up with certain dependent patients who are most likely to generate crises and to make repeated attempts. These patients frustrate our facile formulations and the optimism generated by our success with more conventional patients who do respond to drugs and our ministrations.

New biological approaches must also be explored. The availability of Lithium Carbonate for control of manic excitement and manic-depressive disorders will no doubt have a great impact in the prevention of recurrent depression and, in this sense, in the prevention of suicide since this group accounts for a large proportion of suicides. We are studying the effect of Lithium Carbonate in a group of impulse-ridden patients with repeated, unpredictable and short-lived tension states which often culminate in suicidal behavior. I mention this not to report our success, since we have studied only five patients, so far, but to emphasize the fact that new methods of treatment are likely to jostle our diagnostic habits and lead to re-appraisal of the phenomenological characteristics of the suicide-prone population.

The good fortune of giving a keynote address is the opportunity it affords one to speak in broad terms. I have tried to do this but with attention to some of the existing data and to concrete steps which should be taken. The breadth of the papers to be presented at this multidisciplinary conference and the very existence of this conference attest to significant interest and dedication to this important area of human endeavor, and point to the fact that we have already taken the first step along some of the directions I have just outlined.

2: Social Suicide: Some Neglected Dimensions of Self-destruction in the Megalopolis

Ronald Maris

Not only is it essential to evaluate our professional effectiveness or ineffectiveness with identified suicidal populations, but it is imperative that we learn more about the larger context of destructive social forces in our American society. By identifying those societal elements that affect the individual's life and death we could predict the potentially noxious outcome of the individual's life style and its unintended dysfunctional relationship with society at large. These new understandings must result in change of focus for us all as well as enlarge the sphere of our potential endeavors.

I want to go on record as believing that precision often varies inversely with significance. Many of the really important problems in the arena of self-destruction are not presently amenable to statistical or case-history techniques. One has to be constantly on guard not to let the availability of tools determine the choice of problems. One minor insight into my professional development has been that as I have increased in analytical sophistication, I have had fewer and fewer good ideas to analyze. There is a certain tyranny in "success." Given the real burdens of patient care, supervision of students, grant management, program development and administration, it is all too easy to neglect reading, conversing with students and colleagues about abstractions or entertaining heretical ideas.

15

As a case in point, I would like to argue that one of the neglected dimensions of self-destruction is what we may label "social suicide." More specifically I claim that there are consequences of urban social systems which are unanticipated, unintended, and dysfunctional in that they threaten the equilibrium, and in extreme instances the very life, of the city. A corollary of this position is that suicidologists must not focus attention exclusively on the self-destructive individual. If we wish to identify, predict, and control suicidal individuals, we must also investigate the destructive, synergistic outcomes of individually beneficial system components. Literally, "synergy" means working together. The concept was introduced in sociology by Lester Ward who emphasized that social syntheses were creative; i.e., institutions were qualitatively different from individual behavior or values. Emile Durkheim said much the same thing about social phenomena, when he emphasized that the collective conscience of a society is embodied in no single individual. In synergistic combinations the whole is greater, and often different, than the sum of its parts. Perhaps most importantly for our present purposes, synergy implies that the systemic interrelationships of individually well-intended actions or values, can have unintended corporate outcomes which are detrimental to social order. There are destructive collective social forces as described by the German philosopher Goethe as: "jene Kraft die stets das Gute will und stets das Böse schafft" (that force which constantly wants Good and constantly creates Bad).

For example, in twentieth century urban America we have witnessed the following developments:

—An increasing division of labor.

—Greater interdependency deriving from specialization or occupations and services.

—Higher population density.

—More compartmentalized interaction.

—More instrumental interaction.

—The substitution of law for morality.

—A growing fetishism of industrial commodities and corporations.

—Polarization of racial and ethnic communities.

—Longer life expectancy and increased leisure time.

Allow me to elaborate a few of these developments. The proportion of professionals in the 1960's is three times the 1900 level. Clerical workers are five times as numerous. Laborers are half as numerous today as in 1900. Farmers are one-eighth their turn of the century proportions. Given the increase and diversification of jobs and services, our survival is more contingent upon more people who provide needed goods and services. Comparing 1950 with 1900, twice as many people live in cities of 20,000 or more; three times as many in cities of 100,000 or more. More and more of our social encounters are for resolution of highly specific problems and social interaction tends to be limited to resolution of those problems. Increasingly social interaction is not diffuse, not involving the other person in his avocational roles. Many Black community leaders have urged separatism in their search for identity. Given the prevalent isolation and instrumental interaction the contemporary city-dweller usually does not behave socially out of concern for others so much as out of fear of negative legal sanctions or discontinuance of services provided by others. Finally, in the last sixty years life expectancy has grown from 47 years to 70 years and the work week has shrunk from 55 hours per week to about 38 hours per week.

What has happened when these separate social developments have interacted in urban systems? Without necessarily implying causation let me simply say that today in megalopolises like the Baltimore-Washington, New York City, Chicago, or Los Angeles areas we have large numbers of people forced to live in close proximity and interacting on a depersonalized, professional basis. I believe that this type of interaction is quite likely to be negative. Much of the time one is subjected to detached and dispassionate professional or expert judgments and economic aggressiveness, if not exploitation. Such a situation is tailored to breed alienation and violence or disenchantment and withdrawal. Both of these reactive trends can be regarded as destructive attempts to cope with a hostile environment.

Although on this general level of reasoning it is impossible to specify etiology, let me just remind you of some of the unintended, self-destructive trends in modern city living. Crime rates have risen alarmingly—especially aggravated assault, murder, and (to a lesser degree) suicide. Baltimore, according to one recent report, has become the crime capitol of the nation. There exists, under the rubric of "doing your own thing," a kind of rampant solipsism. One has to question how self-fulfilling narcissistic self-indulgence can be. One of the fundamental tenets of developmental psychology is that it is impossible to be a person without a community. Yet the dilemma is that we have more fragmented and less powerful communities.

Concurrent with increasing crime rates, sexual acting-out, alcoholism, and drug abuse are more prevalent. It is important to stress that these trends cut across social class lines. White-collar crime is less visible but is just as great a problem as blue-collar crime. Anyone who has read John Updike's *Couples* or Phillip Roth's *Portnoy's Complaint* is aware of the confused, chaotic, and empty lives of many suburban dwellers who use sex and drugs to cope with the social developments described above. Particularly in "Couples" John Updike comments on the suburban social treadmill replete with ritualistic week-end activities, "in games" and an empty hangover for Monday morning. The pervasive boredom, meaninglessness and lack of engagement of adults who see themselves as impersonations instead of live human beings attests to the underlying alienation, in our society. The major problem with sexual acting-out and drug abuse is that they are at best short-term evasive maneuvers from underlying social (and individual) pathology. My experience with suicidal patients convinces me that withdrawal or denial coping mechanisms are not useful long-term therapies. Most importantly, sexual deviance and drug abuse are often phases in suicidal careers. That is, they can intensify pathology to the point of an actual suicide attempt or a chronically crippled and unsatisfying existence.

A related dimension of social suicide, which is often neglected, is air and water pollution. In our rush to increase the gross national product, develop technology, and feather our bed of material comforts, paradoxically we have come dangerously close to poisoning whole cities—a kind of social overdose. You are only too familiar with the demise of the Delaware Bay, much of the Great Lakes, the threat to the Chesapeake Bay, the fouling of the sea coasts with oil seepage, heat from atomic reactors, sewage and industrial wastes. Smog from automobiles and industry has intensified problems with lung and respiratory disease of all types. At the present rate of pollution (about 1500 particles per cubic inch per year) it is estimated that by the year 2000 the air will be unfit to breathe and will cause death, without domed cities or individual helmets. The insidious aspect to this pollution is that it is the result of corporate decisions, which are then forced upon the community. However, the situation is further complicated by our desire for industrial goods and services and industry's seeming lack of imagination or will (after all—change costs money) to provide less toxic alternate production modes.

Perhaps the most disturbing aspects of social suicide are the civil and international conflicts epitomized in racial and student riots and the Vietnam War. Dr. Milton Eisenhower, Chairman of the President's Commission on Violence, feels that the most serious threat to the survival of America is our increasing ideological polarization. Blacks are mobilizing against whites (and vice-versa), students are demanding a share of faculty and administrative power, Hawks and Doves are contesting the conduct of the Vietnam War, somehow the generation gap seems wider today than ever before—and underneath all these confrontations lies basically different *ideas* about appropriate life styles. I think one of my clearest exposures to this ideological split came during intermission of a performance of tribal folk-rock musical HAIR in Chicago. One only had to circulate the lobby and eavesdrop on the conversations of rural mid-westerners to appreciate the ideological distances which separate our country. The basic reactions were shock, misunderstanding, and disgust. Values die hard.

All this may seem remote and useless in the identification and treatment of suicidal individuals. Yet I want to suggest that suicidologists should be concerned about larger issues in self-destruction. Furthermore, it is difficult to understand the motivations of suicidal patients if the therapist is not sensitized to the cultural context of individual pathology. In the long run suicide prevention is inextricably bound up with common social values and expectations, as well as legal sanctions for violating those expectations. There are collective, external social forces operating in a system which have unintended destructive consequences. Probably the most successful management of deleterious social consequences and indirectly of suicidal individuals is through reshaping local, state, and federal governmental policy on poverty, education, defense, city-planning, and health. Social policies can kill us. If we do not exercise political responsibility to correct these destructive social policies, we may destroy ourselves.

3: Comments on Suicide among
College Students

Karen P. Blaker

*These three short multidisciplinary papers preceded a
lively audience question and answer period. They sketch
the context out of which each panelist addressed himself
to the theme of identifying suicide potential. Intrapsychic
suicidal risk factors related to feelings of powerlessness,
lack of self esteem and alienation, assume reality when
seen in relationship to the university system and its
transactions with college students or in the self destructive career of the black ghetto resident. They give
evidence of conflicting social patterns interacting with
individual lives. The examination of the inner world of
the therapist working with the suicidal crisis is a fitting
response to the high risk populations described in the first
two papers.*

We have heard from Dr. Maris that the social system in which the
individual functions is one very important variable to consider when
looking at why people commit suicide. I want to focus on the college
student and look with you at one possible kind of interaction
between the developmental needs of the late adolescent and the
social system of the college that may be relevant to the high rate of
suicide among college students.

Suicide is listed as the 10th leading cause of death in the United
States. However, it is now third as the cause of death among youths

15-19 years of age and second among college students.[1,2] Another impressive figure which leads one to consider the college suicide as an important area for action is that quoted by Dr. Matthew Ross, an Associate Professor of Psychiatry at Harvard Medical School. Presenting his findings to the 50th Annual Session of the American College of Physicians, he reported that . . . "in 1966 nearly 100,000 college students threatened suicide, one in 10 of these actually tried it and one in 100, or 1,000 succeeded."[3] Dr. Ross also reported in the same paper that the suicide rate for college students in 1966 was 50% higher than for Americans in general of a comparable age. This figure can be found repeatedly in the literature and is important in answering the question—would the student who commits suicide in the college setting have taken his life under equally stressful conditions outside of college, or is there something inherently stressful for the late adolescent age group in the college social system as it exists today?

In my opinion the dichotomy between what the social system of the college offers and what the student needs may be basic to the high rate of college suicides.

According to Erikson,[4] an individual establishes an identity involving decisions about values, priorities, career plans etc. during his college years. Along with an identity, he must establish intimacy, or a sense of true engagement with other people. If these developmental tasks are not negotiated during these years, transition into a fulfilling adulthood is delayed or perhaps never accomplished.

With these specific tasks to accomplish, it would seem that the student would need a free environment in which to test out his ideas—ideas that will eventually reflect his identity and he will need settings where he can experience relatedness with others.

Instead, he seems to be offered the antithesis of this: Undergraduate classes are often large and impersonal, and tightly controlled in terms of content presented. The curriculum is often so inflexible that in order to graduate within a reasonable time period, the student is forced to decide his life's work early in his college career. We say that the "ideal" student knows what he wants to do even before entering college.

These are unrealistic expectations to impose on college and pre-college students. Unable to find time and an opportunity for discovering themselves as individuals, they feel alienated or isolated from others. And those with the least tolerance for stress, possibly turn to suicide to escape these intolerable conditions.

It could be speculated that the student protest movement on campuses across the nation may be reversing the trend toward making the college student a particularly high-risk suicide group. One surprising statistic on this point appears in a recent study on student suicide at Berkeley.[5] In 1965, the year of the Free Speech (some say Dirty Speech) Movement, there was not one suicide reported on the Berkeley Campus. Very recently Dr. Michael Peck of the Los Angeles Suicide Prevention Center has shown that college students during the past 12 months were *less* likely to commit suicide than young people of the same age outside of college.[6] This is quite a contrast to the statistic reported by Dr. Ross that four years ago the college student was 50% more likely to take his life than his non-college counterpart.

It may be that Dr. Peck has done a tighter statistical study controlling for such factors as age and sex that we know influence suicide statistics or it may be that suicides in the non-college population have increased tremendously. However, we can speculate at least that the rate of college suicide is decreasing. This may indicate that some of the students' needs are being met by the protest movement. Perhaps it provides the opportunity for forging some sort of identity outside what they feel to be a confining collegiate establishment created and run by the older generation. It may also provide a chance for a fuller engagement or intimacy with other students. One could not observe the student occupation of the Columbia University Buildings in 1968 without being impressed by the close interpersonal experience that these students had created among themselves. In short, the student protest movement may help students resolve the twin tasks of identity and intimacy.

It must be added that there are of course, many other variables in every individual's life history that must be considered along with environmental forces in any assessment of suicide potential. However, this paper has focused only on normal developmental tasks of the late adolescent and how they are met and/or not met in a particular social system in our society.

REFERENCES

1. *The New York Times* "Suicide is found second as cause of death among collegians," April 26, 1969.
2. R. H. Seiden, "Campus tragedy: A study of student suicide," *Journal of Abnormal Psychology*, Vol. 71, 1966, p. 389.
3. *New York Times,* April 26, 1969, *op. cit.*
4. Erik Erikson, *Identity: Youth and crisis.* New York: W. W. Norton and Company, Inc., 1968.
5. Seiden, *op. cit.*, p. 399.
6. Personal Communication from Dr. Michael Peck, October, 1969.

4: Suicide among Black Americans

Carlton Blake

It is the purpose of this paper to explode the myth that the suicide rate among the black population is significantly lower than among whites.

It is the author's contention that the high homicide and accident rate with its attendant shortened life expectancy tends to include many suicide victims.

It is well to realize that suicidal intent is concealed in many cases, depending upon the subtlety of the method used and the rigidity with which certification regulations are observed. The law requires very clear indications of conscious intent on the part of the victim before a death can be certified as suicide.

Among the black population, overt suicide is certainly not very common. The predominant defense mechanisms of denial and repression frequently seen when dealing with black patients, perhaps offers a clue to the reason why the overt incidence of suicide is so small as compared to a similar white population.

In working therapeutically with black patients, it is more customary to encounter self-destructive or self-inimical behavior than to obtain verbal statements concerning depression and suicidal thoughts or impulses. Even after the suicidal or self-destruction gesture, there is frequently a pattern of denial, or rationalization of the act.

An examination of the behavior of many very depressed black patients over the years reveals a frequent pattern of withdrawal and resulting neglect of self. When this neglect involves medical care or refusal to continue on life preserving medical regiments, death is frequently the end result; i.e. death due to stroke following untreated hypertension; diabetic comas following untreated hyperglycaemia, and so forth.

Self destructive attempts are sometimes disguised by excessive alcohol ingestion which may have transient psychologically euphoric and ameliorative effect. Moreover, prolonged alcohol toxicity and nutritional deficiency has a progressively destructive impact on health.

Under the influence of alcohol the potential black suicide victim often tends to act out his hostility in a provocative manner frequently inviting self-directed violence on the part of others; i.e. the depressed wife who provokes her husband and when he becomes violent taunts him to "kill me if you want, but I guarantee that both of us will go."

How many deaths occur among the black population labelled as homicide and accidents that are really suicide will probably never be known. A brief review of the homicide and accident statistics for the black population lends great support to this theory, as a result these homicide and accident statistics tend to be inordinately high.

Reality factors such as poverty, ignorance and an oppressive social system have made it, indeed, readily possible for the black man to get himself killed. The acting out of his hostility towards a member or members of the white majority is very likely to result in his own destruction, because of the social climate of racism. A brief review of the recent history of the Black Panther Party will readily confirm this fact. In fact, it was not too long ago that in order to be lynched it was only necessary to assert oneself or to be "uppity" nigger with the white master or his woman.

The black man, therefore, has not had to struggle too much with self-destructive impulses, his struggle has been primarily against the threat of destruction from his social environment. In order to be destroyed, therefore, all that is essentially necessary is to submit to a social system that is well equipped, structured only too eager to produce his dissolution.

It is not at all surprising that overt self-destruction and associated suicidal rates in the black society is recorded as relatively low. History and tradition have forced the black man to develop major defenses against the innumerable social and cultural factors that threaten survival. The breakdown or removal of these defenses almost inevitably results in passive self-destruction. These deaths are recorded as accidental, homicidal or natural, but never as suicidal.

It is obvious that passive methods of self-destruction will prevail in an environment where to destroy oneself simply means giving up the struggle for survival. This is in contra-distinction to self-destruction in an environment geared towards the preservation of one's life, where self-destruction must be a more active process of conscious self inflicted termination of life.

In keeping with this theory, I should like to point out that recent studies show an increase of suicide among middle and upper class blacks which is fast approaching the suicide rates of comparable white groups.

It is the author's contention that the method of self-destruction among blacks will become more overt as the oppressive social and economic factors in his environment are corrected. It should then become increasingly clear that suicide rates among blacks are not significantly different from that among a similar white population. This is, as one would expect since the basic psychological make-up of man does not vary with skin color, or ethnic origin. The variations and overt behavior are in fact determined by cultural and social factors which generally facilitate or inhibit certain types of behavior. Overt self-destructive behavior is no exception to this rule, as one can readily demonstrate by reviewing the recorded overt suicide rates in countries where there are strong religious, moral and ethical prohibitions against self-destruction.

As one who has worked and lived in the ghetto I can assure the reader that things are not always what they seem on the surface. Most black residents may appear happy, complacent or even apathetic but beneath the surface of this relative calm there lurks intense rage and hostility towards their oppressors. Rage which if not expressed is often subtly turned against the black self and any one or anything black. The result is very frequently self-neglect, self-defeat, self-debasement and ultimately self-destruction which is generally recorded in the statistics as death due to accident or homicide.

5: Collected Thoughts of a Suicidologist

Howard M. Bogard

"Do not go gentle into that good night . . . Rage, rage, against the dying of the light"

Dylan Thomas

It would be misleading and capricious to view suicide as a theoretical or metaphysical construct apart from contributing external forces. For, intrapsychic factors are essentially meaningless issues when viewed independently of outside circumstances, happenings or stimuli.

To blanketly and singularly ascribe the etiology of suicide and attempted suicide to an extraordinary instance of retroflected and murderous rage can, in many instances, be reasonably accurate, intellectually stimulating, comforting in its theoretical soundness, and, too often, if one truly searches, disquieting in its dogma. It can also be dangerous, if inappropriately applied.

I do, however, find it rare in the treatment—both successful and unsuccessful—of suicidal patients not to readily perceive omnipotent and chronic rage. Rage related to feelings of rejection, abandonment, loss of status, impotence and, as is so often observed by suicidologists, feelings of helplessness and hopelessness. Reunion fantasies to join deceased parents in death, is but one of a multitude of theoretically and therapeutically meaningful, and at times, valuable, theories. Yet, whatever the nature of the intrapsychic predisposition, it is external forces which trigger the pain, the struggle and the suicidal resolution.

Suicide prevention theorists cannot, on the other hand, direct their concerns to social or external factors alone. For it is just these forces, just this genre of social organization which acts upon the idiosyncratic nature of the potentially suicidal individual. I emphasize idiosyncratic, for I feel that there is no one intrapsychic suicidal predisposition. Suicide is a multidetermined, multifaceted act. And all people do not respond to concrete, readily defined acts, forces and losses in a way which is predictable, absolute, and universal. People respond to representations of losses, not the loss itself. The loss of jobs, love objects and status must be viewed within the eye and the psychology of the individual involved. The loss of a job will mean something far more devastating to a man who has rigorously· overinvested his work.

Should a man's career be part of a compensatory struggle to deny feelings of minimal self worth, loss of his position will set off feelings of failure, humiliation, impotence, uselessness, depression and perhaps of suicide. Thus, if I lose my job, I am nothing . . . if I am nothing I am dead.

Overinvestment in work, career, or for that matter a love object, always tenuously masks underlying feelings of worthlessness. To feel worthless is to feel unloved and unlovable and, as such, better said by Kierkegaard "we stand denuded and see the intolerable abyss of ourselves." Thus with no self esteem and with no narcissism, why live?

Though a multitude of intrapsychic factors can specifically lead to a suicidal resolution, it is always external forces which supply the trigger. One of our immediate concerns is accordingly, are there suicideogenic forces peculiar to certain societies? And, if indeed there are, what can we do? This could be true primary prevention—to minimize the impact of such forces and hopefully eliminate their existence.

On the other hand, we seem to have casually accepted an unquestioned premise. We venture to save lives because suicide is morally, economically and spiritually wrong.

But are all suicides ignoble? What of the altruistic war time hero? What about the soldier who gives his life to save his companions . . . what of those afflicted by terminal cancer . . . why do some suicide, why do others employ massive denial, and others die with grace . . . I do indeed raise the question:

Should their self inflicted deaths be prevented? Can we honestly empathically perceive the physical pain of terminal carcinoma; can we understand the psychological pain, and loss of dignity and narcissism. What of those who gave their lives in the underground during World War II rather than divulge vital information? What of fathers and mothers who consciously sacrificed their lives for their children? Is this selfless sacrifice truly noble? Is this selfless sacrifice truly pathological? Should this selfless sacrifice be prevented?

Do we, in these circumstances, close our eyes, avert our commitment and sing praises to the higher nobility of offering ones life to save another. This then would of course be a very special case and not, within our purview, a true suicide. That is, one that we feel should have been prevented. A true suicide, may indeed write that he dies to provide his family surcease from ministering to his suffering . . . be it cancer or depression. Here we would theorize motives and intra-psychic factors not nearly so noble. What if the life that he destroys is his own and his pain—be it physical or psychological, would thus be removed. Those of you who have shared the agonies of treating severely depressed patients know how debilitating despair can be.

Perhaps, as we so frequently proffer, he can be helped . . . perhaps his pain can be relieved.

My comments are not intended only as those of a devil's advocate. I am also sharing a philosophical dilemma that so rarely is meaningfully confronted and, more often than not, dismissed with a few well worn, however reasonable clichés.

Though I question, I do share an optimism and a life saving purpose. I have saved lives, and this has been something more than just doing my job. I have felt joy and personal satisfaction. Many of us have spent a long night with a suicidal patient. Yet, I have often wondered, when I have permitted myself the luxury of honesty, to ruminate, was I right to have saved this life? Was my wish to save, more important than the patient's wish to die? Have I, because of *my* needs, postponed an inevitability. Have I, because of *our* dedication and even devotion, prolonged intense pain and briefly camouflaged it with tranquilizers, antidepressants and human concern.

Though I feel these questions must be confronted, I nonetheless feel that they are rarely of acute relevance. In a crisis there is no time for soul searching. In such settings I have never equivocated despite my previously confessed introspections. At such times I always feel that the patient can be helped and that his life is precious.

Death is indeed irrevocable, and, as circumstances, wishes, aspirations and availability of love objects can vary and change, there is, more often than not, room for optimism and thus, suicide prevention. If however, people do have the right to take their own lives, as I feel they ultimately do, suicidologists must address themselves to the philosophical and their own intrapsychic issues. For if suicide and mortality holds a morbid, if fleeting fascination for all people—and discussion of suicide and death lead to profound discomfort for most people—why then are there suicidologists?

Generally I do not believe that the nature of the intrapsychic conflicts of those who suicide in western civilization differ at all. Race, cultural traditions, social class and nationality included. Blacks suicide for reasons no different than whites. The wish for love and self worth is ubiquitous. The need to experience another's concern or, if you will, love easily transcends racial lines. Suicidal crises can be successfully managed with minimal theory and much human concern, love and care. Honestly felt reaching out can answer the cry for help.

6: Family Determinants of Suicide Potential*

Joseph Richman

In the context of the conference, this paper followed the very moving experience of the play "Quiet Cries" performed by the Plays for Living group of the Jewish Family Service and served the purpose of moving the focus of the conference from the larger context of social system to that of the individual in a family system. The possibility that suicidal behavior may be conceptualized in terms of a familial system of interaction has strong implications for prevention. If families, at the time of suicidal crises, resemble each other in significant ways, do they resemble each other developmentally? Are we moving toward a point in time when families can be assessed for suicide potential long before the "family drama" of suicide?

In determining the suicidal potential of the individual, we have turned to the people he is involved with, especially in the family, and we have examined the nature of *their* suicidal potential. The term "family suicide potential" refers to those forces in the family structure or family relationships which are conducive to a suicidal act by one of its members under certain conditions of stress.

To identify these family patterns our method consisted of a series

---

* The observations and findings of this paper are based upon a larger work on Suicide and the Family, by Dr. Milton Rosenbaum and the author.

of both individual and family interviews with suicidal persons and their relatives, and a comparison of the interaction that took place with that of a psychiatric control group. The most important procedural point is that one must see the family to know them. It is not enough to hear about the family from the patient or from a third party. It is particularly helpful to see the family in the home. One obtains an understanding there, in the intimacy of the parlor and kitchen, that is not possible in the relative impartiality of the office.

From our observations and experiences we have distilled fourteen aspects of family functioning, all of which have appeared characteristic of a majority of over 100 families with suicidal problems. In this presentation we are only dealing with the family determinants in the present situation, without directly considering the past history, although the effects of early family experiences are certainly implied and at some points touched upon.

The fourteen points are as follows:

1. An intolerance for separation.
2. A symbiosis without empathy.
3. A fixation upon childhood patterns.
4. A fixation upon earlier social roles.
5. A closed family system.
6. A particular pattern of dealing with aggression.
7. Scapegoating.
8. Sadomasochistic relationships.
9. Double bind relationships.
10. Acting out the bad self of the family.
11. A quality of family fragility.
12. A family depression (not only an individual one).
13. Communication disturbances.
14. An intolerance for crises.

These fourteen points describe important areas of family functioning in suicidal behavior. Each one deserves a more extended discussion than we can give it here. The question of which ones are unique to the suicidal family and which are characteristic of emotional or interpersonal disturbance in general is one we are exploring further. Meanwhile, our broad working hypothesis is that they all combine to form a unique pattern, which may be called the suicidal family system.

AN INTOLERANCE FOR SEPARATION

To no one, perhaps, is separation more of a threat than to the suicidal person. Nevertheless, separation is both a constant threat and constantly being threatened, as if there were a compulsion to precipitate the unthinkable. One of the outstanding characteristics of our suicidal families is that they suffer more separation experiences than most—more divorces, more desertions, more deaths, more broken homes, broken love affairs, and broken friendships.

The children in the family fear that the parents will die if they (the children) leave, and so do the parents. The spouses respond to even a minor argument with "I'm leaving," or "Why don't you leave?" But, if a partner calls that bluff and does leave, then the other (or both) becomes suicidal.

Gehrke and Kirschenbaum refer to this pattern as the "survival myth" of the suicidal family. That is, the family must remain intact in order to survive; each individual family member must stay with the family in order to function.[1]

For example, when one daughter announced to the family that she wished to become engaged to be married, the tension rose to such heights that the resulting suicidal act by this daughter or something equally as drastic seemed inevitable. Her older sister had handled the problem by marrying while working in another state and not notifying her family until the marriage was an accomplished fact. The mother then suffered a severe depressive reaction, as she had done when her son was drafted into the army. The father reacted to these multiple but not unusual separations by increasing his already heavy drinking.

In virtually every one of the suicidal subjects we saw the major precipitant of the suicidal behavior involved separation in one form or another, and if it was not a family problem, it was not a suicide problem. These family aspects of separation intolerance assumed several significant forms:

    a. intolerance for separation in general.

    b. intolerance for grief and mourning after a traumatic separation such as that due to a death.

    c. the tendency of the family to become both psychologically and emotionally unavailable to the potential suicide after such a loss.

    d. the tendency of the suicidal person to help set up the conditions for the separation which leads to his self-destructive behavior, and

    e. the tendency for the pattern of separation followed by suicidal reactions to be a repetitive one, love affairs in these persons, for example, are notorious for their unstable and shaky character, with the imminence of separation always hanging over the heads of the partners.

Separation as a fundamental problem is not a recent one, nor is it exclusive to suicidal situations. It is, rather, a universal characteristic of human experience in all places and at all times.

A SYMBIOSIS WITHOUT EMPATHY

John Donne declared that no man is an island entire to himself, that each is part of the mainland. This is a profound and universal truth which might best be understood by those who, like Donne, had met with, faced and transcended the suicidal urge.

In a symbiotic relationship one person can not be seen, and cannot see himself as an individual, but only as part of a larger whole, such as the family, or as an attachment to some other person, such as a parent. If he does attempt to become an individual, dire consequences can follow. Litman and Tabachnick have noted the presence of this pattern in suicidal individuals, and have explained the pathological consequences on the basis of psychoanalytic ego theory. They believe that suicide is symptomatic of some degree of failure in ego development during the separation-individuation phase.[2]

Although in symbiosis two or more units are regarded as one, the relationship is not necessarily a reciprocal one. It appears that in symbiosis people depend on each other for exploitation and satisfaction of neurotic needs rather than for love and cooperation. The exploitative quality is strong and often painful to those observers who have accepted the dictum of Kant that people should be treated as ends in themselves and not as means, or Buber's characterization of the I-Thou relationship wherein a person is related to for himself rather than as an object to be used or studied. The suicidal family, however, is sick psychologically and can do no other.

Within the suicidal family, at the time of the suicidal crisis in particular, there is but a dim or absent recognition of the suicidal person's needs. His motives, for example, will always be interpreted in terms of its effect upon others. A benign example is the statement many fathers will make to their errant sons or daughters, "Look what you are doing to your mother!"

Such a failure in empathy implies a deficiency in the ability to identify or take the role of the symbiotic other, to put oneself in his place and see things as he sees them, combined with the inability to separate. The symbiotic other, therefore, is seen only in terms of oneself. That this is not due to any basic or intrinsic defect in role taking skills is evident when the entire family is worked with. The family members are often very sensitive and able to empathize with others, even if not with the suicidal individual. It is also evident that the family is showing the effect of severe and often chronic anxiety and tension. The anxiety is especially associated with the other becoming a separate individual. It is when this particular type of unempathic symbiosis is threatened that the suicidal person receives the message not to be.

Our investigations not only support the analytic view that the symbiosis is based upon a failure of certain tasks at a very early phase of development, but they also indicate that the early disturbances are maintained by the present system of relationships, and would probably not otherwise continue. We find, too, that the function of these disturbed present relationships is to maintain the pathological early ones. This notion will be discussed further in the section that follows.

A FIXATION UPON INFANTILE PATTERNS

As used in this work, fixation means an attachment to earlier, especially infantile objects, and the use of earlier or immature means of relating in situations or with problems where such fixations are maladaptive. Fixations of course, are not exclusive to suicidal person. Everyone is fixed upon some early patterns that no longer work and where one would be better off rid of them. The problem lies in the number or extent of fixations, how widespread they are, how much of one's functioning is involved, and how much the significant others in one's life are also fixated and therefore strive to keep the person firmly in the same position. The question of the fixation of others is one that deserves wider attention.

Closeness to one's old family or friends would not be pathological in and of itself. But if a married man spent all his time with his parents and ignored his wife, that would suggest a maladaptive infantile fixation. And if his family became upset and his mother ill if he tried to spend more time with his wife and children, that would suggest a *family* fixation upon infantile patterns. The suggestion is that if one member attempted to deviate from this pattern, the others would take steps to restore him to his usual behavior.

In the suicidal person these fixations are widespread, involve a vast amount of his functioning, and the more such territory they emcompass the more serious is the suicidal problem. We believe, moreover, that the fixation is always a family fixation.

Fixations are recognized by two characteristics, their rigidity and their repetitiveness. They appear where some other forms of behavior would have been more appropriate, and they assume the quality of a repetition compulsion.

We believe that early traumatic experiences led to these early fixations and that they are maintained in the present by the entire system of family and social relationships. One goal of the suicidal family, therefore is to foster fixations and prevent change.

Many of the suicidal persons with strong infantile fixations whom we have seen marry partners with similar fixations.

Growth and maturity in many of our suicidal families is equated primarily with separation, loss, and death. The result is a reversal, or even perversion, of the usual values, with growth seen as bad and early fixations as good. To go to school, have friends, work, marry, and acquire a family of one's own are all considered a danger and as occasions for fear. Fixations may be life preserving because change is so unbearable that it may lead to destructive consequences. However, fixation also means failure and conflict. The result is an insoluble dilemma which can be resolved by the suicidal act.

A FIXATION UPON EARLIER SOCIAL ROLES

A role refers to "the function played by an individual in a group," while a status is "the position accorded formally or informally, to a person in his own group . . . . It is always dependent upon the others in the group or community and is partly a matter of how others directly perceive an individual."[3] Although role and status are derived from what others expect and permit, these expectations become built into the individual's psyche, so that the demands of the role becomes what one demands of oneself. The concept is therefore peculiarly valuable for dealing with individuals in their social settings.

The suicidal family is more concerned with social recognition or failure, and more dependent than most upon social acceptance and position in school, work, peer relationships, sexual relationships, and in the family. The entire area of social role and status, therefore, is a most sensitive one for the detection and correction of suicidal potential.

In our own studies of role functioning in suicidal persons[4] we evaluated the role adequacy of suicidal and nonsuicidal persons in six areas where social role competency is vital. These were work, school, peer relationships, sexual relationships, role as spouse and role as parent. In addition, as a rough measure of role development with time we also obtained a rating of the degree of separation from the original parents or family. We found the following features.

A pattern of role disturbances and role failure pervaded every area of social and personal functioning, and these role disturbances were always embedded in a family pattern of role disturbances. We found a family pattern in which roles were frequently fixated, often reversed, with a preponderance of passive fathers (or else sadistically brutal ones) and domineering mothers who were themselves infantile and mother attached. We emphasize, therefore, that the role difficulties involve all members of the family, and in most cases the family needed to have the suicidal individual a failure in meeting the usual role expectations.

The fathers of the younger suicidal patient were often related to like a sibling or contemporary of their children, rather than as parents. There was often a sexualized attitude towards the daughter and a rivalrous one towards the son. For example, the father of one boy attributed his son's suicide attempt to depression and chagrin at seeing his father receive a job promotion while he, the son, was a failure at work.

The mothers often related to the suicidal girl as to a mother, sister, or lover. One mother spent hours telling her daughter of her experiences at work and with friends. She acted like a rejected suitor when her daughter, in her 20's, acquired other interests and activities.

The families we saw exhibited what DeVos[5] called role narcissism, meaning an undue stress upon social role to the detriment of true individuality. The role narcissist is what he appears socially and has little other identity. The role narcissism and stress upon appearance fostered the secretiveness of the family. It was often used punitively, with the potentially suicidal person exposed to public ridicule and taunts.

The fixation of the family members upon earlier family roles and the parents upon premarital ones was the most prominent feature. Our clinical data highlighted the inability of the family members to change roles with physical growth and mental development, and especially to move from a childhood to a more mature status. The parents have remained in the role of children in their own families of origin, and their children repeat this pattern when they marry.

Past and present combine to maintain these pathlogical role relationships. We found, that the function of the current disturbance is to maintain the earlier, though now outmoded, roles.

Finally, the necessity of a change in roles as a result of the inexorable demands of fate and life is the spur which elevates the intensity of the role conflicts to suicidal proportions.

These first four categories, the intolerance for separation, the symbiosis without empathy, the infantile fixations, and the failure of role development, are clearly subdivisions of the problem of individuation and development.

A CLOSED FAMILY SYSTEM

A "closed family system" refers to a family that cannot tolerate any outside contacts that would threaten to change its established structure. A friendship by a member, for example, with someone whose standards or habits are different, a confidante who may encourage an unwanted independence, a fiancée who wants to establish a new and separate family unit, are examples of such threats. Such friendships and contacts are therefore broken up, and the family closes itself off.

As the mother of one suicidal son confided, "If someone loves my children or my parents very much I get to dislike that person." One suicidal person after another has described their parents and siblings, as well as themselves, as excessively and often fanatically jealous.

Such a sealing off never occurs in a firm and well stuctured unit. It only takes place within a group whose weaknesses render it particularly vulnerable and threatened by change. Although the suicidal families we have seen are closed in the sense we have described, they are amorphous and poorly bounded. There is a lack of autonomy and clear cut boundaries to the nuclear family and a lack of separation from the extended family and families of origin of both parents. The older generation is inordinately involved, and always in a destructive and divisive way. When the older generation is not destructive then the family is not suicidal.

We commonly observe that the family tries to prevent the potentially suicidal member from making outside contacts. That is one reason the Suicide Prevention centers do not reach the most suicidal persons. When close ties do develop they are often destroyed, even if self-destruction is necessitated. We have frequently seen much suicidal behavior in patients in therapy which arose out of the family's distress at the person forming an intimate relationship with an outside-the-family other. The family which can tolerate such relationships, on the other hand, is oriented towards life and continued growth and not towards suicide.

AGGRESSION AND DEATH WISHES DIRECTED AGAINST THE POTENTIALLY SUICIDAL PERSON BY THE FAMILY

Freud, and others since, placed emphasis upon the aggression of the suicidal person against others,[6] which becomes turned against himself. That there is aggression against the suicidal person which plays a role in his act has also been recognized by several recent writers, including Meerloo,[7] Maddison and McKey,[8] and Jourard.[9]

We found that a pattern of marked hositility directed against the suicidal person by his family was prominent. For example, death wishes, verbalized or expressed in nonverbal and indirect forms, occurred with unexpected frequency in the families of our suicidal population. It is not only his own aggression which is turned against himself by the suicidal person, but also the accumulated aggression of others. This pattern is often covert and indeed the opposite of the manifest picture. A sibling or parent will side with the suicidal person when alone, for example, but turn against him when the other parent or some other centrally significant and pathological person is present. That, incidentally, is one reason why it is so advisable first, that the therapist see the entire family, and second, that he be familiar with the principles of basic family dynamics and interviewing.

All this is not to infer that the suicidal person can not be aggressive or hostile. The suicidal person's hostility is such, however, that it always bounces back upon himself. In addition, the suicidal person is more often inhibited, quiet, and relatively less hostile than those in his surroundings.

To sum up a very complex dynamic picture, aggression in suicide can best be understood as part of a pattern of dealing with imminent or threatened change; a pattern which differs, according to our observations, from those in people who develop other psychiatric disturbances or who overcome their difficulties. The suicidal person we saw was someone who expressed feelings that he was a burden to others who were fed up with him and who would be better off if he were out of the way. The other family members we saw expressed similar feelings, that they *were* burdened and that the suicidal person *was* too much for them. These feelings and attitudes occurred in a closed family system, as we have described, which forbade the person to seek contacts on the outside, so that he had no outlets for his aggression and no allies. Aggression, therefore, appeared as an extremely important variable, but one that could best be understood in the context of the total pattern of relationships.

SCAPEGOATING

As used in our studies, the scapegoat is the family member who is held responsible for the difficulties encountered by the family. He is to blame.

On the whole, the suicidal family can be characterized as blamers. This sometimes adds to the problems in treating the suicidal person: the treatment may be effective, but nothing is really altered. If attitudes towards the suicidal person become more positive the family then simply finds another family member to blame, and that someone may then become suicidal. For example, one alcoholic man who had made a serious suicide attempt, agreed to join AA and go into psychotherapy. His wife reacted by becoming depressed and tearful and said, "Maybe I'm at the bottom of all this drinking and *I* should go away someplace." Apparently someone had to be the blameworthy person; if not the alcoholic husband then the bad wife. Often one finds that a series of persons become suicidal, for example, each child as he becomes an adolescent and strives towards greater independence.

The punishment and scapegoating we have seen in the suicidal families have assumed the following forms:

A major form is the punitive isolation of the suicidal person and his alienation from the rest of the family. The danger of suicide in such cases is high not in the schizoid, isolated individual, but in the dependent one with a strong need for love and closeness. When such a person is in a crisis, therefore, and is being progressively and effectively made the recipient of all blame and anger, then the likelihood of a suicidal act is great.

Another frequent punitive measure, already mentioned, is *public humiliation.* Criticism and ridicule of the person in front of his friends is frequent.

The shameful exclusion of the person from functions where the family was open to public view is another scapegoating measure. When one woman became married, for example, her mother was not invited and not permitted to attend because her daughter feared she would make a scene. She would be embarrassed, explained her daughter, adding that she was ashamed of her mother, who, incidentally, subsequently killed herself.

SADOMASOCHISTIC RELATIONSHIPS

Sadomasochism refers to a pattern of interpersonal relationships characterized by an alternation between hurting and being hurt. Frequently this pattern exists in the context of a symbiotic relationship. Most suicidal families that we have seen fit this description, illustrating that sadomasochistic relationships are not necessarily limited to two people. Furthermore we are implying that this characteristic interaction seems to be handed down from one generation to another. Let me give an example to illustrate the reciprocal nature of this behaviour pattern.

The wife of one young man announced that she had fallen in love with his best friend. The husband's response was "In that case I'll not stand in your way," as he walked out of the apartment. Feeling lost and abandoned he hung around the house for hours. After seeing his wife's paramour enter, he experienced a strong urge to kill himself.

Panicked, he ran to another friend who brought him to the emergency room of the hospital. His wife was contacted and came immediately. In the subsequent interview with both of them, the husband explained that he expected his wife to call him back when he walked out. Her response was "After you left I was as close to killing myself as I have ever been in my life!" The episode was characteristic of a marriage which emerged as a running sadomasochistic battle.

DOUBLE BIND RELATIONSHIPS

The double bind we are here referring to is a particular ambivalent relationship in which neither distance or closeness can be tolerated, but where the person or persons involved receive messages to be both distant and close simultaneously, and then are punished no matter what they do. This pattern is analogous to the "double bind" communication concept of Bateson et al.[10] In double bind communications a person may receive two conflicting messages simultaneously to which he cannot respond without being punished and neither of which he can escape.

In the typical suicidal family everyone has what can be described as a "barbed wire" exterior, so that anyone coming close is hurt, yet no one can tolerate distance. Thus, no matter what the relationship, it is impossible to meet the mutual needs of each family member; which leads to conflict, strife, and self-destructive behaviour. Again this pattern seems to be perpetuated in other relationships. The suicidal person from this kind of family usually chooses a spouse or lover who exhibits the same familiar behaviour. He seems destined, therefore, to enter into one impossible double bind after another, which in a context of sufficient hostility and scapegoating, can take a suicidal turn. The moral seems to be: If you would perpetuate an impossible situation, use impossible methods.

THE SUICIDAL PERSON
IS THE "BAD OBJECT" FOR THE FAMILY

The case records of suicidal patients in Jacobi Hospital are dotted with such comments as "For as long as she (the patient) can remember, she has been viewed as the "bad" person in the family." We have evidence that in some cases the suicidal person is acting out the forbidden wishes and impulses of the parents, and therefore represents the bad self of the family, which has to be punished. The collective guilt is then expiated through the suicidal act.

The pattern is allied with the scapegoating proclivities of the suicidal family, and could be considered as one aspect of scapegoating. It is not only in suicide, of course, that we see one person acting out the forbidden needs and wishes of another, but the history of the maltreatment of the suicide by church and state suggests that the suicide could represent the bad object of society at large. The vampire legend arose through the custom of burying a suicide at a crossroads with a stake through his heart. In literature, Mr. Hyde and Dorian Gray are certainly graphic examples of suicide killing off the bad object or the bad self.

Not only is he seen by the family as "bad", but the suicidal person himself, feels responsible for all the ills of those he loves. One adolescent girl said all her family's problems were the result of her mental illness. A sixteen year old girl reported that as she was swallowing a bottle of pills, "I felt I was somehow saving my father; but I don't know why." The schizophrenic patient, in our experience, is usually considered "sick" by his family; while the suicidal person is labeled as "bad".

A QUALITY OF FAMILY FRAGILITY

A suicidal family sees itself as inadequate to meet the demands of every day living or the stresses of change and development in its various members. If one parent is potentially suicidal he may be seen as fragile and incompetent or these traits are considered proof of his or her essential badness. If the potentially suicidal member is a child, then both parents may be seen as fragile and in need of protection by that child, rather than persons from whom one can expect parenting. For example, a sixteen year old boy experienced urges to go to the roof of his apartment house and jump off. He finally came to the psychiatric emergency rooms seeking help. He felt he could not turn to his parents and refused any suggestion that he do so, because his mother had asthma and any upsetting situation would precipitate an attack, while his father reacted to any pressure by becoming uncontrollably excited and leaving home for several days.

The view of the parents as fragile and unable to function on their own is part of the family myth in the suicidal family. Moreover, in our observations, this is a very deep rooted myth, and the entire family as a result labors under so much tension, anxiety, fear and depression, that they have few resources for dealing with change and challenge.

A FAMILY DEPRESSION

The suicidal family is often exquisitely vulnerable to depression and has the unhappy facility of including death in areas which are merely problems for other families. Combined with this preoccupation with death is an apprehension over loss and the annihilation of the self, all of which is aggravated by any threat of change. Yet family members live in despair of their life as it is. Frequently the frankly suicidal person in the family is identified with or symbiotically tied to a depressed parent. One mother, for example, profoundly depressed, unable to care for her home or leave the house, took to her bed, preoccupied with money worries and death. Her twenty-two year old daughter developed the same symptoms, but attempted to leave the house. The ensuing argument with her mother was followed by the daughter's suicidal attempt.

The depressive family concept suggests a need for further investigations of the relationship of the suicidal person with a depression-producing other, both past and present. The interpersonal approach to depression has been neglected in research and clinical study to date in favor of a more intrapsychic examination of the dynamics and evaluation of depression.

COMMUNICATION DISTURBANCES

Suicide is itself a communication. It is a cry for help, an appeal to others, a method of retaliation or revenge, an expression of atonement and a confession. For our purposes, communication refers only to direct or indirect messages, either verbal or nonverbal, relevant to a suicidal act.

The published literature indicates that up to seventy-five percent or more persons who killed themselves communicated their intent in advance and that these communications were recent, repeated, and expressed to many persons.

In our population the difference between those psychiatric patients who did or did not attempt suicide did not necessarily lie in the presence or absence of suicidal ideas. The differences lay in a variety of situational, personal, and interpersonal circumstances, including how the suicidal feelings were received by others, the actual suicidal stress or danger of the situation, and the messages communicated to, as well as from, the suicidal individual.

What has been largely overlooked, in studies of the communication of intent is the reciprocal, two-way nature of communication. One example was that of a woman in her forties who had made repeated suicide attempts in the past ten years, following the tragic death by accident of her son. She was seen in a family interview following one of her attempts, during which the interviewer asked if she ever tried to tell anyone how she felt. She replied that she tried to tell her husband that she was depressed on the night before her latest attempt, but that he had ignored her. (As she was talking her husband turned away from her.) He then explained that as an intellectual, he had been reading and had no time for trivial conversation.

In an examination of all the case histories we have seen, suicidal families are characterized by some typical communication patterns. Frequently, for example, there have been overt expressions by relatives of death wishes and other messages that the potential suicidal family member do away with himself. There also seems to be an imperviousness or non-reception to verbal messages from the suicidal person by the relatives. Deliberate isolation and ignoring of the suicidal member, particularly when he is voicing suicidal thoughts occurs. Often the suicidal person is cut off when talking or reacting, and told that he has no right to express his thoughts or feelings. The nonverbal gesture of turning away or turning one's back on a significant other is a repeatedly observed habit in suicidal families. Thus, not only is the suicidal family characterized by a paucity of dialogue, a tendency towards rejection of mutual communication, an emphasis upon secretiveness and isolation of the suicidal person, but access to sources of communication *outside* the family are also forbidden. It is a lethal bind in every way.

AN INTOLERANCE FOR CRISES

We have noted in our suicidal families that the factors which contribute to a suicidal reaction frequently come to a head under the impact of family and developmental crises which affect the usual patterns of all normal families. Anything which threatens the suicidal family's homeostasis constitutes a crisis.

A scapegoating and destructive reaction to crises seems typical. Changes, such as seen when an adolescent starts dating, or an older man retires, necessitate a change in attitude and behaviour in other family members. Even in families where a suicidogenic situation had a long history, we found the most frequent immediate circumstance leading to a suicidal act was a family conflict resulting from a change or attempted change in the assigned role of one member of that family.

An example is that of one man in his mid-twenties who was treated more like a thirteen or fourteen year old by his parents. He had always been a "good" boy who was a companion at home and confidante for his mother. When this ideal, obedient son began going out, returning late, and not confiding in his mother, he became "bad". He arrived home at three a.m. one evening and was met at the door by his enraged and sleepless parents. A violent quarrel ensued which was terminated when the boy stabbed himself in the stomach.

In the above case the suicidal crisis erupted in the context of a delayed adolescent reaction which lead to an unbearable level of tension, anxiety, depression, and rage in both the parents and the son. With older persons the crisis situation is related more to the vicissitudes of aging. One man in his mid-seventies became disabled and dependent upon his wife for physical care. She refused to obtain outside help yet was not physically or emotionally equipped to deal with the change. Unable to care for himself and unwilling to continue as a burden to his wife he cut his throat one day when she went out shopping.

A POSITIVE CONCLUSION

The suicidal gesture can perform a positive and sometimes essential social task. It communicates the need for changing a poorly functioning system of family relationships in people who are caught up in a mutually destructive situation. Frequently it is the only means available for signaling the need for change and improvement. The suicidal act is therefore not only a cry for help and not only a collective as well as individual cry for help; but is also an opportunity that should be utilized for its potential for positive change.

It is all too easy to become so caught up in the emotional difficulties, disturbances, conflicts, stresses and tensions that beset the suicidal family that the more loving, tender, and caring components are overlooked. Nevertheless, it is as important to evaluate the positive potentials as the negative ones: to see the successes as well as the failures of families. What is needed is more investigations of people and families who affirm life against odds, of those who exhibit life-enhancing behaviour in contrast to life threatening or self destructive behaviour. No one has studied those people with a history of early parental loss and family disorganization, who reacted with growth, maturity, and better living!

Working with suicidal families is often exasperating and terribly anxiety provoking—yet we have also found that working with these families and discovering and reinforcing their *life-saving potential* can be the most rewarding experience one can encounter.

In the near future we hope to use the family behaviour patterns described, to construct an assessment guide for the identification of suicide potential in families.

REFERENCES

1. Gehrke, S., & Kirschenbaum, M. Survival patterns in family conjoint therapy. *Family Process,* 1967, **6,** 67-80.
2. Litman, Robert E., & Tabachnick, Norman D. Psychoanalytic theories of suicide. In H. L. P. Resnik, (Ed.), *Suicidal Behaviors: Diagnosis and Management.* Boston: Little Brown and Company, 1968, Pp. 73-81.
3. English, Horace B., and English, Ava C. *A comprehensive dictionary of psychological and psychoanalytic terms.* New York: Longmans, Green and Co., 1958. P. 522.

4. Richman, J. and Rosenbaum, M. A clinical study of role relationships in suicidal and non-suicidal psychiatric patients. Paper presented at the Fifth International Conference on Suicide Prevention, London: September 25, 1969.

5. DeVos, George A. Suicide in cross-cultural perspective. In H. L. P. Resnik (Ed.), *Suicidal behaviors: Diagnosis and management.* Boston: Little Brown and Company, 1968, Pp. 105 -134.

6. Freud, Sigmund. Mourning and melancholia. *Collected papers, IV,* London: Hogarth Press, 1946, Pp. 152-170.

7. Meerloo, Joost A. M. Suicide, menticide, and psychic homicide. *AMA Archives of Neurology and Psychiatry,* 1959, 81, 360-362.

8. Maddison, David, and McKey, Kenneth H. Suicide: The clinical problem. *British Journal of Psychiatry,* 1966, 112, 693-703.

9. Jourard, Sidney. The invitation to die. In E. S. Shneidman, (Ed.), *On the nature of suicide.* San Francisco: Jossey-Bass, 1969, Pp. 129-141.

10. Bateson, Gregory, Jackson, Don D., Haley, Jay, & Weakland, John. Towards a theory of schizophrenia. *Behavioral Science,* 1956, 1, 251-264.

BIBLIOGRAPHY

Breed, Warren. Occupational mobility and suicide among white males. *American Sociological Review,* 1963, 28, 179-188.

DeLong, W. B., & Robins, E. The communication of suicidal intent prior to psychiatric hospitalization: A study of 87 patients. *American Journal of Psychiatry,* 1961, 117 (8), 695-705.

Dorpat, T. L., & Boswell, J. W. An evaluation of suicidal intent in suicide attempts. *Comprehensive Psychiatry,* 1963, 4 (2), 117-125.

Easson, William, M., & Steinhilber, Richard M. Murderous aggression by children and adolescents. *Archives of General Psychiatry,* 1961, 4, 1-9.

Gibbs, J. P., & Martin, W. I. *Status integration and suicide.* Oregon: University of Oregon Press, 1964.

Henry, Andrew F., & Short, James F., Jr. *Suicide and homicide: Some economic, sociological, and psychological aspects of aggression.* New York: Free Press, 1954.

Johnson, Adelaide M. Sanctions for superego lacunae of adolescents. In K. R. Eissler (Ed.) *Searchlight on delinquency.* New York: International Universities Press, 1949. 225-245.

Kessel, N., & Grossman, G. Suicide in alcoholics, *British Medical Journal,* 1961, 268, 1671-1672.

Klein, Melanie. The psychogenesis of manic depressive states. In *Contributions to psychoanalysis, 1921-1945.* London: Hogarth, 1948.

Leonard, Calista V. *Understanding and preventing suicide.* Springfield, Ill.: Charles C. Thomas, 1967.

Lonsdorf, Richard G. Legal aspects of suicide. In H. L. P. Resnik (Ed.) *Suicidal behaviors: Diagnosis and management.* Boston: Little Brown and Company, 1968. 135-143.

Murphy, George E., & Robins, Eli. The communication of suicidal ideas. In H. L. P. Resnik (Ed.) *Suicidal behaviors: Diagnosis and management.* Boston: Little Brown and Company, 1968. 163-170.

Pokorny, A. D. Characteristics of 44 patients who subsequently committed suicide. *AMA Archives of General Psychiatry,* 1960, 2, 314-323.

Richman, J. Family determinants of attempted suicide. In N. L. Farberow (Ed.) *Proceedings of the Fourth International Conference for Suicide Prevention,* 1968, 372-380.

Richman, J. & Rosenbaum, M. The family doctor and the suicidal family. *Psychiatry in Medicine,* 1970, 1 (1), 27-35.

Robins, E., Gassner, S., Kayes, J., Wilkinson, R. H., & Murphy, G. E. The communication of suicidal intent. *American Journal of Psychiatry,* 1959, 115, 724-733.

Robins, E., & Murphy, G. E. The physicians' role in the prevention of suicide. In L. Yochelson (Ed.) *Symposium on Suicide.* Washington, D. C.: George Washington School of Medicine, 1967, 84-92.

Rosenbaum, M., & Richman, J. Suicide prevention in the military. *Military Medicine,* 1970.

Rosenbaum, M. & Richman, J. Suicide: The role of hostility and death wishes from the family—A preliminary report. *Proceedings of the 77th Annual Convention of the American Psychological Association,* 1969, 4.

Rosenbaum, M. & Richman, J. Suicide: The role of hostility and death wishes from the family and significant others. *American Journal of Psychiatry,* 1970, 126 (11) 1652-1655.

Rosenbaum, M., & Richman, J. The role of hostility and rejection by society in suicidal behavior. Paper presented at the Fifth International Conference on Suicide Prevention, London, England, September 25, 1969.

Tabachnick, Norman D. Interpersonal relations in suicide attempts: A psychodynamic formulation and some indications for treatment. *AMA Archives of General Psychiatry,* 1961, 4, 16-21.

Watzlawick, Paul, Beavin, Janet Helmick, & Jackson, Don D. *Pragmatics of human communication.* New York: W. W. Norton, 1967.

Part Two

It is often postulated that within the social order we tend to perpetuate existing systems rather than move to change elements of the systems which by their nature alienate the high risk populations. If this holds true, then how can the human service professions, themselves traditional systems, radicalize to affect destructive forces in our way of life?

In the following five papers the authors deal with specific areas of primary and secondary prevention from their own professional perspective. These include a conceptual frame of reference, the nature of interpersonal responses to the "germ of destruction," the profound difficulties of survival among alcoholics, the relationship of the cleric and the sick person, and the low risk caller.

7: Primary and Secondary Prevention: A Frame of Reference

M. Leah Gorman

How can the principles of Preventive Psychiatry be applied to suicide? Concepts of primary and secondary prevention will be examined for applicability to the field of suicidology.

Ronald Maris suggests that suicide is not an isolated social problem but rather it is an act of deviance which hangs together with a whole system of deviance.[1] Related social problems such as drug addiction, alcoholism, homicide, and mental illness fall within an *entire system* of deviance which is self-destructive. Suicide then cannot be studied in isolation from other social problems.

We have sufficient evidence to suggest that the act of suicide although the most dramatic and the most final, is but one of several alternatives arising from faulty interactions between man and his social environment. Prevention of social deviance is hampered not only by complex theories of multiple causation, but by the fact that it is easier to overlook the indirect effects of human experience than to overlook the more immediate and visible ones.

When the final outcome of human experience is as dramatic as suicide, we are most likely to forget the complexity and diversity of the process with which we are dealing.[2]

It is for these reasons, among others, that priorities in community mental health continue to focus on the acts of deviance rather than on the more subtle and more complex processes which underlie them.

Suicidologists report that in spite of increases in the numbers of suicide prevention centers in the country, the suicide rate has not decreased, but has in fact increased! Are we overlooking a vital dimension to suicide prevention? I am referring to a dimension which recognizes the relationship between the amount of community integration and the effectiveness of mental health services. The more community integration, the more effective services and vice-versa. Preventive efforts must be directed toward modifying those social forces which lead to community disintegration and which in turn influence the processes leading to self destruction.

Archaic institutions which no longer meet their clients' needs, alienation of groups of people from the mainstream of society, and enforced early retirement are examples of *disintegrating* social forces which can and do lead to acts of deviance.

Primary prevention, as defined by Caplan, is a *community* concept which involves lowering the rate of mental disorder in a population by counteracting harmful circumstances before they've had a chance to produce illness.[3] Inherent in the primary prevention model are two interrelated directions for action; the first is in improving those non-specific 'helping resources' in the community, and the second relates to reducing those environmental conditions in the community which we have reason to believe are harmful to man. The *community* is the focus in primary prevention. It is only through the associations and the institutions of the community that interpersonal supports become a reality to people. Erich Lindeman in his studies on acute grief underscores this point in his assertion that it is the community which gives rise *both* to the hazards of living and to the potentials for successful coping.[4]

Primary prevention work to date has been pretty much confined to improving the helping resources of the community. The helping resources of a community are frequently referred to as gate-keepers. The term, gate-keepers, used loosely, refers to those formal and informal helping people, who by virtue of their occupational and/or social position in the community are frequently in contact with people. Such gate-keepers, to mention a few, are clergymen, doctors, bartenders, policemen, teachers, and nurses. It is believed that the kind of help offered to an individual by a gate-keeper can have a major effect in determining his choices and his ultimate outcome.

Organized professional efforts have been directed toward increasing the formal gate-keeper's effectiveness by ensuring that we have the necessary knowledge to detect incipient signs of disaster.

I seriously question whether the means of such preventive efforts justify the ends. Are we not perpetuating the status quo of malfunctioning institutions? To equip a 'keeper of the gate' with sufficient knowledge to detect suicide potential, for example, could in itself reinforce a system which subtly invites suicide by the process of dehumanization. A frequent response to a rash of suicides by prison inmates is to provide an educational experience to help prison guards detect the early signs of suicide. This approach by omission rather than commission sanctions an archaic system which perpetuates unhealthy relationships between man and his social environment.

The very act of creating new roles and new programs within antiquated systems enables existing professional groups to continue their work as before and thus to avoid the discomforts of disrupting the status-quo as inevitable in planned structural change.[5] It is also undoubtedly easier to add new roles and new programs than to modify the basic structure of our institutions.

A question which looms large in relation to primary prevention is whether or not we have sufficient etiological evidence to warrant modification of social forces. Caplan suggests that while we are waiting for further results of etiological research, we may still achieve success in primary prevention by exploiting our present, less-than-perfect knowledge.[3] For example, we know that college students have a higher suicide rate than non-college students of the same age. We also know from psychiatrists who are dealing with youth that they are seeing much anxiety over the failure of the adolescent to define for himself the adult role he wants to fill. In addition to these two factors, college youth are telling us loudly and clearly that the traditional modes of constraint in our colleges are no longer useful either in ensuring group cohesion, structural interdependence, or regulations for behavior. How definitive do our etiological findings have to be before preventive priorities are directed toward correcting the harmful effects of institutional decay?

Mental health professionals are indeed caught in the horns of a dilemma when it comes to primary prevention. As Klein points out, if the professional is too zealous in searching out the basic causes of community disorganization and social malfunctioning, he is liable to suspicion if not censure by the power structure.[6] Members of the helping professions are not usually in the best position in the power structure of the community to implement social reform. Perhaps then, the question becomes, in what new ways can the professional bring his knowledge to bear on the problems of community disorganization and social malfunctioning?

To date, preventive efforts in the primary mode have been largely in the direction of increasing helping resources rather than in modifying noxious social forces. This is true not only in suicide prevention but in community mental health preventive work across the board. The greatest concentration of preventive work is seen in the secondary mode. Secondary prevention refers to the activities involved in reducing the prevalence of a disease entity by casefinding, early diagnosis and intervention. Programs of secondary prevention emphasize not only the traditional problems of diagnosis and treatment, but also the logistics of maximum use of resources of workers and of knowledge.

We've heard that prevention centers tend to be called primarily by those individuals in the populations with low suicide potential. In one city it was found that less than 2% of the completed suicides had previous contact with their suicide prevention center.[2] Does this mean that some groups of people in the community do not have access to information about available health resources? Does it suggest that the nature of services offered is seen as unhelpful by some segments of the population? How, then can we bridge the gap between our existing services and those people in the community who do not see them as useful?

I have emphasized primary prevention in this discussion because secondary prevention, although terribly necessary, connotes to me an 'after-the-fact' kind of intervention. The 'fact' representing an individual already in a crisis situation. Until we can actualize the goals of primary prevention, mental health workers will by necessity be deploying their expertise in the secondary mode of prevention.

In conclusion I raise a further question; can we develop an overall strategy of suicide prevention which will combine and actualize the goals of the primary and the secondary mode?

REFERENCES

1. Maris, Ronald, *Social forces in urban suicide,* Homewood, Ill.: Dorsey Press, 1969.
2. Shneidman, Edwin, *On the nature of suicide,* Jossey-Bass, Inc., San Francisco, 1969.
3. Caplan, Gerald, *Principles of preventive psychiatry,* New York: Basic Books, Inc., 1964.
4. Parad, Howard J., *Crisis intervention: Selected readings,* Family Service Assoc. of America, New York: 1965.
5. Leighton, Alexander, "Poverty and social change," *Scientific American,* May, 1965.
6. Klein, Donald C., *Community Dynamics and Mental Health,* New York: John Wiley & Sons, Inc., 1968.

8: For Whom the Id Tolls

E. Alden Ellison

In trying to prevent something it is helpful to estimate the forces at work. Where mortality factors are concerned, a division into two categories can be made; those that are self-spreading and those that are self-contained. A death agent may succumb to different methods of control, depending on whether it multiplies itself or works in isolation. Thus, for example, reduction in cardiac mortality, the number one killer, and deaths from pneumonia and influenza, fourth on the list, would seem to be problems that are unalike. Medicine has characteristically had more success in controlling contagious diseases. A glance at the mortality table for 1900 shows the leading agents were influenza and pneumonia, tuberculosis and gastro-enteritis. Today, only penumonia and influenza remain, much reduced in incidence.[1]

In this country, where suicide is concerned, the rate differs little from 1900 (10.7 vs. 10.2 per 100,000). Yet it has had its ups and downs, rising to 16.8 in 1908 and 17.4 in 1932. Within this national average, there are wide geographical variations. San Franciso's rate has been as high as 45 and Rhode Island as low as 3.8. One is at least tempted to think: endemic and epidemic.

Can suicide be classed as a communicable disease? Certainly not in the conventional sense that a germ is to be isolated and a suitable immunization discovered. Yet in another important sense, that suicide is self-propagating, it may be so. It is well known that suicide is higher when the individual comes from a family in which suicide has occurred. In the 1960's, in S. Vietnam, self-immolation staged as a planned political instrument was followed by so many unconnected suicides that Buddhist leaders publically admitted the situation was out of control.[2]

A more intimate glimpse into this phenomenon of transmission comes from the 18th century. A book published in Germany in 1774 touched off a mass reaction throughout Europe and claimed the life of many a person. The author, later to pen another work of high impact, *Faust,* had written a novel called *The Sorrows of Young Werther.* Translated into many languages, and the first European book to appear in Chinese, it had a universal appeal; Napoleon carried a copy during all his campaigns and in 1808 met with Goethe to discuss its motivation. Servant girls were found with the book in their pocket after suiciding. A French traveller to England remarked that he could not go abroad of an evening without seeing a dead body afloat or hanging from a tree. The alarming increase of suicides led to denunciations of Goethe from the pulpit and to his own effort to reverse the trend by writing a play, "The Triumph of Sensibility". In the background of this phenomenon lay a personal experience. Goethe had fallen hopelessly in love with the wife of a friend. In despair, he withdrew from the situation and considered suicide. At this point, a friend beset with the same problem found a solution by borrowing a pistol from the woman's husband and killing himself. This also solved Goethe's problem: he could either follow suit or "complete a poetic task in which all I felt, thought and fancied should be put into words".

The result was the story of Werther, a young man hopelessly in love with the wife of another, who borrows a pistol from the husband as a suicidal weapon. Goethe felt better: "by writing this book I saved myself from a stormy element, felt once more happy and free as if I had made a general confession. But while I had gained freedom, my friends went astray thru my work, thinking they must change the fictitious into the real and in any case blow their brains out. What thus in the beginning took place among a few afterwards happened in the great public, and this little book which had been so useful to me got a bad name as being highly pernicious".[3]

What impact does this have for those who deal with troubled people? It indicates something of the magnitude of the problem. A rough estimate of 10 attempted for each completed suicide suggests that we accumulate within our population a ¼ million people each year and in a decade, about 2½ million who have tried suicide.[4] Knowing that previous attempts increase the potential for completed suicide, and bearing in mind the seductive effect of suicidal behaviour, the presence of this vast suicide pool in the population becomes slightly awesome.

This communicable factor also has an impact for those dealing with the individual bent on suicide. Relatives not infrequently remove psychiatric patients from the hospital despite the doctor's clear warning of suicide intent. Perhaps this may be simply a failure in prevention or there may be something more lethal about it. Patients who have nearly succeeded at suicide are often enough restored to consciousness and discharged from the hospital over the alarmed protest of relatives. This could be due to lack of bed space but may reflect a kind of reaction toward people who carry the germ of destruction.

Several studies of completed suicide groups indicate that a sizeable percentage had consulted a physician in the period from 6 months to the day of suicide, and not a few had utilized prescribed medicine as the suicide instrument. The suspicion of collusion here is not undermined by recalling that the suicide rate among physicians is considerably higher than the general population, and among psychiatrists is higher still. One might reason that most suicides suffer from depression, that depressed people are more apt to complain of physical symptoms than the depression, and in any event seldom volunteer their suicidal thoughts. Overlooking suicide potential might then be simply a diagnostic error. However, the cardinal signs of depression are too well known. It is much more understandable that failure of recognition results from a kind of emotional stoppage.

The forces at work in a potentially suicidal person are powerful, all pervasive and not at all agreeable. With some modifications and additions, the original insight that no person suicides who has not first felt homicidal impulses, is valid dynamically. Herbert Hendin, in a recently published study of black suicide in New York City,[5] has demonstrated this anew in a remarkable series of cases. The clinical material shows that the Negro, in trying to cope with his rage, consciously hovers between homicide and suicide, as compared with the White, in whom the process is largely an unconscious one. The supporting statistics accord with this: black suicide in the 20-35 age group is twice that of whites and coincides with the peak in homicide. Among whites, the incidence of homicide and suicide tends to vary inversely.

One is dealing then—no matter how covered over—with anger of the most violent sort, along with that indicator of dangerous situations, anxiety. The anger may arise out of a variety of life situations but is in any event there to be dealt with in some fashion by the therapist. And here is met with a difficulty. The universal reaction to anger is counter-anger—no matter how covered over—and this is also true of anxiety. That such feelings are not at all agreeable to the therapist and could significantly affect his perception, judgment and utilization of skills is not hard to conceive.

This sometimes issues in an avoidance of the situation, or, less politely, the patient is rejected. It is reasoned that to inquire about suicidal thoughts is to open the way to suicidal action. The physician who refused the coroner's request for information about a patient on the grounds he did not have the patient's permission, must surely have felt that in silence lies no violence. If the patient is nominally accepted, he may be treated with an overprescription of medication and an underprescription of the physician's self. But particularly when treatment is entered upon and there begins that long, gruelling working-through of intense feelings, the unremitting emotional bombardment of the therapist, is the likelihood of counter-reaction greatest. Suicidal patients require protracted, unlimited and dependent relationships, and this can weigh heavily on the therapist, who is not immune from depression and consequent identification with the patient. A study of 20 completed suicides by patients in an Eastern State Hospital concluded that the doctors' behaviour had strongly influenced the patients' behaviour. One group of doctors with records of treatment failures had "quiet, friendly, noncompetitive character make-ups. They let themselves be manipulated and led astray by sentiment in cases where there was a need for control and accurate rapid therapy. There were repeated and needless postponements of unpleasant therapy measures, changes in orders and decisions, and prolonged hesitation. It was inevitable that sooner or later a patient would perceive this lack of direction and realize that actually he was on his own". The other doctor group was found to have "pronounced, sharpedged personalities which require considerable expenditure of energy for control of aggressions. Their involvement in patients' problems was limited and routine and seemed to indicate a cynicism towards the possible benefits of therapy".[6]

That the "therapist" is here referred to as "doctor" is simply to employ a convenient generic term. The dynamics are the same for any worker in suicide prevention. That a person highly trained is not always immune to communicable dangers might be slightly depressing to a beginner or someone with less training. Yet there is some comfort in all being in the same vessel and more importantly, in something else.

What is spoken of here is referred to in some circles as counter-transference, in others as "keeping one's cool", and in still others as the enjoinder to "know thyself". I suspect they all refer to the same thing—that much of what we do, or do not do, is determined by the degree of awareness of what transpires in ourselves. That few physicians would knowingly reject a patient goes without saying. That many a person in distress is unkowingly turned away by friend, relative or professional is also clear. It was not so long ago that the word suicide had the same taboo as venereal disease.

The fact is that the potential suicide does not know that he is angry, or depressed, or anxious. And so he labors at a tragic disadvantage. He needs help, and indeed, may not survive without it. The therapist has to face the fact that his most important instrument is himself, that he too is capable of these same feelings, that they can be stimulated by contact with such a person, that he is dealing with a communicable danger, that he must be interested and understanding, but need not and should not assume the patient's emotional burdens. Else, like Goethe, we may arrive at something therapeutic for ourselves but unprofitable for the patient.

REFERENCES

1. Linder, F. and Grove, R. *Vital Statistics Rates in the United States, 1900-1940,* Washington: U.S. Department of Commerce, Bureau of Census, 1943.
2. N. Y. Times, *Budhist to Student Priest Suicides*, Aug. 14, 1:7, 1963.
3. MD, *Literary Lament,* 13, 202-206, Nov. 1969.
4. Resnik, H. L. P., The neglected search for the suicidococcus contagiosa, *Archives of Environmental Health*, Sept. 1969.
5. Hendin, H. Black suicide, New York: Basic Books, Inc. 1969.
6. Rotov, Michael, Death By Suicide in the Hospital, *American Journal of Psychotherapy*, 25, 2, 216-227, April, 1970.

9: Suicide in the Alcoholic Population

LeClaire Bissell

There seems to be very little doubt that there is a profound relationship between alcoholism and suicide. Studies from 12 countries and summaries of 20 papers[1] point to the incidence of alcoholism in suicidal populations as ranging anywhere from 6-39% depending on the population and the research design. Some are studies of completed suicides, others are attempted suicides and the term alcoholic is rarely clearly defined. In Kessel's study from Edinburgh of 501 consecutive admissions to a poisoning treatment unit[2] 39% of the men and 8% of the women were described as alcoholic. This is one of the better papers in that Kessel fortunately tells us what he means by alcohol addiction, specifically that physical signs were present. Most authors fail to do so. In Blachly's recent study of completed suicides among eighty physicians[3], it is interesting to note that 39% were described by their next of kin as being heavy drinkers or alcoholic and that 19% were actually drinking at the time of their death. There is obviously a need for clearer statistical information. The figures available on traffic accidents, may or may not also reflect suicidal intent; 40% or 50% involve at least one heavily drinking individual, and of those who are chronic repeaters, most turn out to be alcoholic. The people who burn themselves up in their armchairs or beds, the pedestrians who stumble in front of cars, in each of these categories the incidence of alcoholism is extremely

high. So, although we know few exact figures, or how many are
intentional suicides, there are far too many of them.

Not only do we need more accurate studies relating to frankly
suicidal behaviors of alcoholics, but we need valid studies of
behaviors of individuals addicted to combinations of drugs as well as
to alcohol alone.

In dealing with alcoholism, most authorities agree we are facing a
chronic progressive and ultimately fatal disease which can be arrested
but very rarely cured in the traditional sense, if by "cure" we mean
that the individual returns safely to social drinking. This is not a
realistic therapeutic goal. We are dealing with a disease of extremely
high incidence. A recent estimate is nine million Americans[4]. Seen
in a more meaningful way, one out of every 15 drinking adults is or
will become an alcoholic. The term alcoholic often conjures up the
stereotype of the end stage alcoholic. This is rather like thinking
about cancer only as a terminal metastatic condition and waiting
until one arrived at that state before calling it cancer.

Alcoholism does not begin in a Bowery doorway or with delirium
tremens. It does not start in a divorce court or a jail or at the first
hospital admission. These are already rather late sequelae and many
alcoholics are diagnosed, treated and recover without experiencing
any of them.

I think we have to look at our own attitudes about this, and realize
that we are part of a Puritan culture in a Puritan land where
alcoholism is still regarded as a moral problem or ecclesiastical
disorder of some sort, rather than an illness. Part of the problem is
that the alcoholic is seen as being irresponsible (and his behavior
often is) and as having fun (which he most certainly isn't!). If
alcoholism is that much fun, we have to ask why the victim of this
carefree disease kills himself rather than continues with it. We
continue to hear statements "but George can't possibly be an
alcoholic, because after all he doesn't drink in the morning and he
always goes to work, and he supports his family and besides he wears

a clean white shirt and was in college with my brother." What this means is that George is not seen as an alcoholic because he is not yet terminal. The vast majority of alcoholics never arrive at Skid Row. The Bowery population represents less than 3% of the total. The other 97% are living in the larger community, or rather they are dying among us. Insurance companies are quite matter of fact about this. When they discover that a person is alcoholic they simply scissor off 12-14 years of his life expectancy and adjust their premiums accordingly. Alcoholics are dying in our midst under diagnoses that mask the alcoholism. In hospitals you will find them categorized as cirrhosis, pancreatitis, or peripheral neuropathy—or acute and chronic brain syndrome, or anemia or G.I. bleeding, or esophageal varices, all of these often being consequences of the disease of alcoholism. Thus hospitals continue to treat alcoholics all of the time but are rarely treating the alcoholism at all.

Menninger wrote about alcoholism as a form of slow suicide. Shneidman has referred to alcoholism as a way of "playing dead." It is tempting but inadequate to view alcoholism simply as a substitute for suicide or as an alternative, for alcoholics commit suicide in large numbers in very conventional ways, quite distinct from their drinking. They shoot themselves, they take pills, they deliberately run their cars off the road.

For the suicidologist who is looking for clues of depression to assess lethality, the physical side effects of alcoholism are hard to separate out. Questions relating to sleep and appetite disturbances, and changes in bowel habits are inaccurate indices when asked of the heavy drinker. High alcohol consumption depresses the appetite. Sleep disturbances are chronic with the alcoholic. Alcohol has two effects; the initial sedative effect is followed some hours later by an excitation stage. A very heavy drinker going to bed at 2 A.M. after 8-10 drinks is going to wake early the next morning. A severely addicted alcoholic is going to wake up every 4 or 5 hours at night, and will combat the excitation from the drinks of 4 or 5 hours ago with more drinking. Alcohol has all sorts of effects on the G.I. tract, so that one will find periods of alternating constipation and diarrhea in an alcoholic population.

Is the alcoholic depressed? A classical way of viewing alcoholism regards it as symptomatic of underlying emotional pain or depression. The next step then would be to find the cause of the pain or tragedy, deal with the underlying pathology and hope that the alcoholic symptoms would disappear. Since alcoholics are often unable to cooperate with the usual psychotherapeutic approaches, this is frequently an unsuccessful type of treatment. In addition, the consequences of severe alcoholism are ample cause for a reactive depression. For example, the patient who arrives in the hospital for detoxification, although he may arrive drunk, may sober up to confront the fact that he is broke, his wife may have walked out, he may be losing his job, his medical insurance premium may have been unpaid—who wouldn't be depressed? Frequently, this situational depression lifts after the patient has been in the hospital for a few days. We have also noted an unexplained but transient depression after the third or fourth month of sobriety—a phenomenon where more accurate data collection is indicated.

Primary prevention of alcoholism is virtually impossible. We know that Prohibition was a failure. Mandatory education about alcoholism in the schools is most unsuccessful, at least with the teaching methods now in use. Good secondary prevention may be our best recourse. Early recognition and intervention has been shown to be highly effective but we must overcome our reluctance to do it.

Let me give you an example. Let's say you are a nurse, working on a floor in a general hospital. There are two other nurses working with you and you see them daily on the unit and when you give the four o'clock report. One of those nurses has a very severe cough which she's had for two weeks. You listen to this and note that it doesn't improve. I would guess that before the third week has passed, somebody in that group of nurses is going to say "Hey! Mary Jane, that is a terrible cough, why don't you go to a doctor and have something done about it?" Now let's set up another situation. You're in exactly the same group, but with you is another nurse, who has begun to miss mornings on duty, particularly mornings after she's had two days off. She has recently broken up with her husband. She's had several rather hard to explain minor injuries. Some months ago she fell at home and broke her ankle. She says she's been mugged a time or two and several members of the family have died so that she has missed work. There have been a few episodes; a staff party, where really she did overdo it a bit; she had people in for dinner, when she didn't feel well and passed out at the dinner party so the guests had to go home early. Little things are happening. Someone may have smelled something on her breath; but then again maybe she had the flu; maybe that was just terpin hydrate she was taking for a cough. The signs can be every bit this glaring and I will bet you that every single other nurse on that nurse's station is going to surround this woman with a conspiracy of silence, join her in her own denial, refuse to look at the problem, refuse to confront her; ultimately when she gets fired or is admitted after an overdose, then everyone's going to cluck and say isn't it too bad, but of course it's because she had such an unhappy childhood and we really couldn't have done anything anyhow. Nonsense! I think we have to look at what's right under our noses—I think we have to look at this problem—I think we have to find out something about alcoholism because it's one of the most common diseases we've got in our midst. Now who's going to treat it? *We are,* the entire lot of us, because again, let's say that we agree that psychiatrists should treat all alcoholics, that only psychiatrists could do it. If I could take all the psychiatrists away from Suicidology, take every last one of them out to California and put them to work doing nothing but treating alcoholics in California, there wouldn't be enough to go around for California's alcoholics. This would be assuming that psychiatrists wanted to treat alcoholics and were standing in line for the privilege. They're not. They are obviously not the answer, alone—and to say "I am not a trained psychiatrist" or "I don't have a Ph.D." is to a great extent a cop-out! AA came into existence 35 years ago, founded by a physician and a stockbroker to fill the vacuum left by the professionals. So far it is still doing a more effective job than most of us are doing in the health professions.

There are one or two cardinal rules in dealing with alcoholic patients. The first one is, if you can't treat the alcoholism, at least don't make it worse. Don't cross-addict the patient to another drug. One of our biggest problems in dealing with this group is not the sensible use of slow-acting mood elevators, or the phenothiazines; but it is the random cross-addiction of the sleepless alcoholic to Doriden, or Librium or Valium or barbiturates or Noludar or Quaalude. Don't put the instrument of his own self-destruction into the alcoholic's hands! The second rule is to get familiar with community resources available to you—read something about alcoholism. Marty Mann's book "New Primer on Alcoholism" is excellent as a starter.[5] Know your local AA group—you are welcome to visit it. Know it, go there, meet some of the people so that when you have the distressed alcoholic in your office you can get on the phone, call up somebody and say, "Ed, I've got a nice guy here, his name is Bill—I'd like you to talk to him right now." Make the contact, hand him the receiver, and get out of the room!

REFERENCES

1. Public Health Papers No. 35, World Health Organization, *Prevention of Suicide*, Geneva: 1968, Pp. 66-67.
2. Kessel, Neil. Self poisoning. In *Essays in self-destruction*, Edwin S. Shneidman, (Ed.), Chap. 16, Science House, New York, 1967, p. 359.
3. Blachly, P. H., Disher, Wm. & Roduner, Gregory, Suicide by physicians. *Bulletin of Suicidology*, December, 1968, Pp. 1-18.
4. Egeberg, Roger O., Assistant Secretary for Health, Education and Welfare, as quoted in an article by Jane E. Brody, New York Times, April 5, 1970, p. 47.
5. Mann, Marty. *New primer on alcoholism*. Holt, Rhinehart and Winston, Inc. New York, 1958.

10: A Hospital Chaplain Views Suicide

Robert B. Reeves, Jr.

A story may make a good point of entry. A fellow walked into one of what we call the "Avenue churches," forgetfully left his hat on, walked all the way to the front row, and sat down. After a little while one of the ushers came down and tapped him on the shoulder. "Pardon me, Sir," he said, "you've left your hat on." The gentleman looked up, smiled broadly, took his hat off, and said, "Thank you, thank you. I've been coming here for twenty years and this is the first time anyone has spoken to me."—Which may say a whole lot more than anything else I could say, about the contribution our churches are making to the reasons why people take their lives.

From the angle from which I approach the problem, which is that of a hospital chaplain, who works with people hospitalized for acute medical difficulties, I see the overt and specific act of suicide as the final capping piece at the top of a whole pyramid of covert and symbolic behavior. We often speak of suicide as if it were a form of sickness. I speak of most sickness as a form of suicide.

We know of the dehumanization and the alienation that takes place in our society. Whenever the conditions of life become intolerable, because of crowded population, impossible living conditions, old age, sickness, misery, vocational or personal or family problems that people can't cope with, in most human societies in the past, and many in the present, there has been a way out. Certainly that is the case in non-human species. Lemmings take care of it, when they

75

outgrow their means of subsistence, by leaping off cliffs in frenzied thousands. The Eskimo who feels that he has become a drag upon his clan quietly goes off and cuts a hole in the ice. The African bushman in similar circumstances goes off into the jungle, takes a potion, and lies down to sleep beneath a tree: the ants do a clean job. The Japanese honorably resort to Hari-Kari.

Where it is acceptable in a society, or when a species has learned to survive as a species this way, we do not call it suicide, we do not give it an invidious name. Where, however, a society regards it as unacceptable, a tremendous number of people, for whom life has become intolerable, are inhibited from resorting to any of these overt, specific ways of ending life. Instead, we may see mass violence, the kind of massive self-destruction that takes place in a riot; or we may see it on the highway, or in alcoholism, or on the drug scene. We may see it take place symbolically at a place like Bethel, where people are drowned in sound—a lovely way of drowning!

Or people do it by getting sick. I cannot prove this—it is speculation pure and simple—but I suppose that the majority of people we admit at Presbyterian Hospital are there because in one way or another life has become intolerable. They are too well controlled to take any of the other ways out, they have too high a regard for social taboos to kill themselves, they are too fastidious perhaps to take the alcoholic route, they can't behave as lemmings. So they come up with disease. This is not to say that disease is psychogenic. I do not mean that at all. Rather, I mean that people become sitting ducks for whatever bugs or falling bricks are in the air around them.

Family Researchers have said that suicide seems to be less frequent among the psychiatrically sick than in the rest of the hospital population. Truly, psychosis is a kind of death to an intolerable life situation, so there is less need for overt suicide. Similarly, there are relatively fewer suicides among cancer patients than in the general population, because cancer itself becomes the suicidal course. Sometimes, when we successfully cure people, we deprive them of sickness as an out, and leave them then no course but overt suicide. I have known a number of patients, whose neurotic conditions or physical ailments were cleared up, who then had no way to symbolize their suicidal tendencies, and ended up by performing the overt act.

The institutions of religion have played a big part in bringing about this state of affairs. Many people have found that their religion, instead of contributing to their love of life and love of self, their ability to love others, their self-esteem, their sense of worth, their feeling of being wanted—instead of giving them fulfilling relationships,—has tended to isolate them, judge them, condemn them, drive them in upon themselves, despoil them of the satisfactions of outward reaching. And when they go to church or synagogue for help, as they so often do, they are, in Dr. Ellison's words, "overtreated by prescription and undertreated by the self of the helping person." They are told to pray about it, or to attend church more often. The rituals are resorted to, the traditional formulas are trotted out; and a fellow can go to church for 20 years and nobody talk to him, until, when finally someone does tap him on the shoulder, it's "Thank you, thank you."

We need in our church life—although in a metropolitan center like this it is something that concerns only a minority of the people, across the rest of the country it concerns a much greater proportion—we need to recover the kind of climate in which people are so cherished that they can learn to love themselves. You cannot love your neighbor unless you love yourself. This is the kind of thing that builds back and forth: as you learn to love self you can love others, as you love others they in turn learn to love themselves, and life for all becomes enhanced.

In the absence of these fulfilling relationships, a person loses his sense of being in convenant with life. In the absence of a sense of covenant with life, anything that comes along that gives a person a way out, at either a conscious or an unconscious level, that is the way he takes. I have no statistics as to the incidence of suicide among regular church goers, but I do know that at one period some years ago in the City of Seattle, which probably has more neon "Jesus Saves" signs per square block than any other city in the land, the suicide rate was the highest of any city in the land. And I wonder if the kind of religion indicated by neon signs and slogans, and the fundamentalist theology behind them, with its over-riding of human values, didn't have something to do with it. Of course, you might argue another way: Seattle has the greatest rainfall—maybe that's what caused it!

As I see my task, it is not to sell people a religious bill of goods, it is not to say whether or not they are theologically correct. As a matter of fact, I am not concerned whether they consider themselves "saved" nor not. I want to know, can this human being find comfort in himself, can he live with himself, is he in touch with himself, does he like himself?

In terms of primary prevention, if I can get through to this person in a way that says, "Okay, I value you," maybe he then can make the projection and say, "Well, if this fellow can, who is supposed to be a minister, then maybe God values me too." But if I start preaching at him and say, "God values you, therefore hold your head up," it's no good, no good; the preaching gets in the way. People find God only through other people. Read the letters of John! If in pastoral treatment I do not convey to the person who is on a downhill course that he is worth something to me, then all the ritualizing, the sacramentalizing, the preaching is just so much wasted effort.

The only way that people through religion are going to find help in whatever kind of suicidal course they are embarked upon, is to experience cherishing by other people. If we could get rid of most of the real estate we are encumbered by in the church, so we could stop worrying about raising money to maintain it, and pay attention to people; if we could get rid of all the prestige-seeking, the jockeying for position, the concern for status, and start tending to people; maybe we could begin to pull our weight in society again, and maybe we could begin to find again in our fellowship in church the kind of fulfillment that would let us say to one another, "I like being here with you." That is the only thing that ever saves anybody.

I see a great deal of fine professional practice in our shop. Some of it carries this note of caring, some of it does not. As I trail around behind the various attending physicians and residents, and see the people they are seeing, I can almost always pick up whether or not the relationship is truly a helping relationship. Where it is a helping relationship, it doesn't seem too much to matter as to one course of treatment against another. Something takes place in the patient that creates a favorable response to whatever treatment he is getting. Where there is not this kind of cherishing relationship, staff can pull heroics until they are blue in the face, and the patient continues on his downhill, suicidal course.

My plea would be for religionists especially, and for those with related concerns, not to pay too much attention to whether people are theologically right or wrong, or whether they perform the rituals or not. Rather, get back to basic human concern. Develop among people the kind of relationships where they can say, "It's good to be here with you." That is the road to salvation, and the answer to so many of these potential suicides.

11: What Can We Learn from the Low-Risk Caller to a Suicide Prevention Center?

Lenora McClean

The fact that the majority of callers to a suicide prevention center are people who are at relatively low risk has been substantially documented by the records of such centers across the country. At the National Save-A-Life League in New York, callers assessed at high risk make up approximately one-third of the nearly two hundred callers weekly; that is, they are considered most likely to kill themselves in the very near future unless intervention takes place. Among the other two thirds of the callers assessed at moderate to low risk, or those who are less likely to kill themselves in the very near future, are people with a vast assortment of complex problems and whose coping mechanisms are often minimal. Also in the population of low risk callers are those people who are significantly different in the way they identify themselves. Usually, callers do not quickly divulge their thoughts of suicide without the help of the counselor. By contrast, these callers that I see as different almost invariably preface any personal data by saying, "I'm not suicidal yet, but . . . ." This is usually followed by the contingency that if things don't change for them suicide will become the only remaining alternative.

I will address my thoughts about prevention to this group of people primarily because they leave me baffled and fascinated by the possibilities they might afford us, to learn more about suicidal phenomena and to explore innovative approaches to prevention.

A brief profile of these callers to the National Save-A-Life League will serve as a point of reference. The caller is usually female, unmarried, between 25 and 35 years of age. Her perturbation is not acute and she is well integrated. She is not addicted to alcohol or drugs although a significant person in her social environment may be. She is usually focused on a specific problem which is stressful but some pervasive difficulty may be affecting her life. She is a middle-class wage earner; she may or may not have had psychotherapy and she has never attempted suicide. A significant characteristic of this caller is that she sees herself on a destructive course in life. Usually, this perception of herself and her life has emerged gradually after continuous efforts to overcome frustrations have failed.

While the profile serves to pull together a number of salient commonalities of many callers, a brief description of such a caller may communicate the complexity of the problems they present and thus clarify my concern.

> Miss A. was referred to the National Save-A-Life League by a friend in whom she had confided that if something didn't "Give" in her life situation, "One of these days I'm gonna go and take the kids with me," i.e. kill the kids and herself. Miss A. was talking about the life she is leading: she is a strikingly beautiful Black woman, aged 35, working part-time as a model, part-time as a practical nurse, and caring for three children, given over to her by a younger sister who spent considerable time in prison for shoplifting, prostitution, and dealing in drug traffic. Miss A. "managed" on her income, even saved money from time to time, until her sister visited, upset the children by threatening to take them away, and demanded money from Miss A. who reluctantly yielded in order to send the sister away and restore peace. At the time of her friend's concern, Miss A. needed day care for the youngest child, a pre-schooler, so she could work full-time, better health care for all four, and she was anticipating another "visit" by her sister.

My normal pattern of response to this type of caller involves exploratory interviewing which subsequently takes a supportive, problem-solving course usually ending in referral for some help with the problem or problems causing the most stress. Miss A. knew what some of her most stressful problems were and what kind of help she needed. However, she did not know that there were resources in her neighborhood for both day care and health care that were within her budget. Additional referral for legal advice regarding her status with the children and their natural mother and therapy for herself gave her several new ways to manage the stress in her life. When follow-up is accomplished it usually reveals, as with Miss A., someone who has more control in her life and she has a somewhat more optimistic outlook.

Though this is far from the tense drama of rescue often fantasized as typical work in the suicide prevention center, I would like to believe it is an investment of time and energy well spent. Yet, I have only questions about these callers. Who are these people, really? Are they people who are not potentially suicidal, people who are struggling with difficulties but are somehow being sustained by the struggle? If they are not suicidal, why did they call? Could the fact that they call a suicide prevention center for help be due to the action orientation of the center? That is, are these the sort of people who are able to identify resources for action when action is needed at crucial points in their lives? If this is the case, then the possibility of ultimately resorting to suicide may serve as the leverage needed to get help.

On the other hand, are these people potentially, or pre-suicidal, and if so how could we learn about the process? With close followup and systematic evaluation could we identify a stage of breakdown in a progressively destructive life style? Could we learn how suicide is selected as an alternative? If these people are indeed pre-suicidal, then as a population they would offer excellent opportunities to study self-destructive processes, possible reversibility of such processes, and the opportunity to test and implement much of the knowledge we have gained from data left by people who have committed suicide.

Regardless of the eventual suicidal potential of this group of callers, one thing seems patently clear: the kind of help that is sought is not crisis intervention which is thought to be the mission of the suicide prevention center. Rather, it is some sort of supportive consult-and-advise, or problem-solving help that may well come under the prevention umbrella somewhere between primary and secondary.

Confronted with these kinds of needs, it seems essential to conceive of reasonable ways of meeting them and not necessarily within a suicide, or crisis center. I believe the future resources to operational-ize prevention of suicide and other gross mental health problems are groups of lay volunteers. For example, why not extend the concept of the indigenous worker to the indigenous lay volunteer who would be trained in problem solving and consultation skills. It seems that such helpers may be able to respond both to needs for sincere, caring human resources and for realistic help in tapping necessary organiza-tional or bureaucratic resources that exist but appear somewhat remote or alien from the person in need. Miss A. had obvious needs for day care services and health services and through the League resources were found to meet these needs. However, Miss A. still needs people to care about her and upon whom she can call to "talk things over."

Teams of lay volunteers might serve as community reference groups, or work in mobile units, or work in collaboration with churches, synagogues, community centers, block associations or in some other sustaining structure to provide problem clinics or some other means of relating to needs of the respective community. At a time when much of the population is so ready, in fact, demanding involvement of people and coming to grips with problems, such a thrust into the community beyond the suicide prevention center may really begin to reach and alter illness and suicide statistics.

Summary

The fact that suicide rates in this country have not been appreciably lowered by the recent burgeoning interest and growth of suicide prevention centers, was the springboard for every paper presented at the conference. It served as the primary challenge to consider innovative approaches, to identifying suicidal intent which became the unifying mandate to the entire multidisciplinary group of people who attended. It obviated the necessity to work together in a community of committed human beings and to learn as much as possible about the phenomenology of suicide in America.

Around this central theme of lack of effectiveness in suicide prevention, papers seemed to fall into two categories: Those that expanded understanding of the nature of self destruction in high risk individuals such as alcoholics, college students, blacks, and inter-actional relationships with familial and societal suicidogenic factors; and papers that suggested a creative treatment approach, an innovative use of a different helping population, or simply a confrontation of some sacred cows of traditional suicide therapies and their disastrous effects.

Self destruction took on global stature when described as a pervasive phenomenon in the wanton pollution of our environment, the persistent defeat of gun and firearm-limiting-laws, the civil strife and the endless military conflict. It could be conjectured that the self destructive life style of the high risk individual who found himself at the nexus of entrapping familial or societal forces was in a predictable condition. Contrary to being "master" of his fate, the suicidal individual could be more accurately described as a victim.

Health professionals were variously seen as victims too, of professionalism, established hierachies and perpetuated "helping" postures. However this view was counteracted with the warmth and human concern of the therapist who sits up all night with his patient—only to ask himself "Am I right? Am I really helping by intervening."

Repeatedly, we were confronted with indications of need for different and more aggressive detection and prevention processes. For example: the alcoholic who is cross-addicted to barbituates and other drugs by a well-meaning physician; the black diabetic who breaks clinic appointments and refuses insulin; the chronically ill, elderly shut-in; the family with the myth that one of them will die a violent death. In the tradition of the Suicide Prevention Center, better named Crisis Center, one should not wait for this person to call, because calling is not part of his personal repertoire. We must seek him out—a reversal of traditional behavior, but essential if we mean to affect suicide rates. Some unconventional suggestions from the participants were ways of "drawing out" and engaging isolated people such as the single room occupant, preparation for retirement in industry; the use of the elderly in helping roles; and the honest confrontation of alcoholic friends who are traditionally surrounded by "conspiracies of silence."

QUESTIONS IN DISCUSSION

What About the Aged?

Senior citizens were well represented by one of the panelists on the second day of the conference. Their spokesman, Mr. David Rachlis, Field Service Coordinator, National Council on Aging, pointed to the increasing number of elderly in our country and the pressures of enforced idleness, lack of financial income, and increasingly poor health, all of which adds up to disengagement dependency, and lack of resources. It is not surprising that suicides in the over-50 age group constitute about one fourth of all suicides in the country. Even though the elderly are a largely untapped resource of experiential and accumulated knowledges, the aged in our country have been treated as an unwanted minority.

Who is Responsible?

Gate-keepers are all those formal and informal helping people in the community —ministers, teachers, nurses, police, doctors, bartenders, the list is endless and may include every responsible member of a community. The need is apparent that not only traditional gate-keepers are responsible for being helpful to others, but perhaps a revival of the concept of being one's "brother's keeper" is in order. Certainly it is evident that we need to work toward rehumanization of the human service professions as well as other aspects of our technological society so that sensitivity to human needs remains a part of our personal and social make-up.

Do We Have the Right to Intervene in Suicide?

Rhetoric abounds on this question and there are some very real philosophical issues involved. Unfortunately, however, philosophizing often serves to rationalize lack of involvement with others, or helps us placate our feelings of frustration, helplessness, and anger when we are faced with frustration and failure. Until rhetorical questions have realistic answers, do we have the right *not* to intervene?

"Though they sink through the sea
They shall rise again;
Though lovers be lost, love shall not
And death shall have no dominion"
                                        Dylan Thomas

D.A.
L. McC.

Appendix

Information Giving as Adjunct to Treatment

Ari Kiev

Inasmuch as there is a great need for public education regarding suicidal behavior, and an equally great need for the appropriate involvement of family and friends with suicidal persons, the following material is in response to these needs. This material forms the basis for two hand-outs given to patients and their relatives attending the Suicide Prevention Clinic at the New York Hospital-Cornell Medical Center. They are particularly useful in providing a broad framework for understanding the problems of mental illness and its management. They have been edited in order to be more generally applicable to other Suicide Prevention Centers or Crisis Clinics.

Guidelines for Friends and Relatives
of Psychiatric Patients

Ari Kiev and Cathleen Greene

It is important to recognize the effects of psychiatric illness or a suicide attempt on friends and relatives of the client. These effects can range from incapacitating anxiety and dread, which can complicate the person's problems, to helpful, useful responses which can speed his recovery. Spontaneous fears that nothing will be the same or that the client will get worse sometimes occur. Setbacks, or a zig-zag course, may create more tension and doubts about the value of the treatment, and intensify the indecision and fear from which he already suffers. By contrast, intelligent, supportive attitudes can bolster the client's confidence and hope, and can sustain him through the depths of despair.

We believe that friends and relatives of suicidal people who become psychiatric patients should learn as much as possible about the treatment they are receiving; the effect of the medicine being used; what to expect in the way of progress and setbacks; how to help the person with decisions about responsibilities and new activities; and how to cope with their own feelings during the course of the illness.

This Guide contains answers to some of the questions most frequently asked by relatives and friends of suicidal persons. Although each person's problems require individual solutions, the suggestions here can be of much use for friends and relatives in their day to day dealings with him.

91

WHAT KIND OF TREATMENT DO PERSONS RECEIVE IN A SUICIDE PREVENTION CLINIC?

Usually the rapid reduction of symptoms is the most immediate goal. This is accomplished with the help of antidepressant and tranquilizing medications which have been developed in the past fifteen years. These medicines are particularly effective in alleviating the symptoms of psychiatric illness with a minimum of interference with daily functioning. This makes it possible for clients to continue their usual routines in the community, who in the past might have required hospitalization.

Simultaneously with this stress on symptom relief, a program of re-education of the client is begun. This program is based on the assumption that positive changes in an individual's life adaptation can take place at any point in his life and that growth and development are not restricted to the early years of life.

With the active participation of the staff, the client reviews his recent life experiences, relevant past experiences, and most important, the nature of his relationships with other people. The focus is on the present and on ways to improve daily functioning. The client's awareness of personal habits which may contribute to difficulties with others is increased. He is encouraged to reassess his goals, assets and liabilities, and to work toward developing better ways of coping with stress and relating to others, which will maximize a sense of security and satisfaction.

Clients are told about the basic nature of their illness so that they can recognize the early symptoms of recurrences and obtain prompt help. As in the treatment of physical illness, early treatment can prevent the more serious complications of psychiatric illness.

AM I THE CAUSE OF THE SUICIDAL PERSON'S DIFFICULTIES?

The mood and behavior of people with psychiatric illness are often distressing and difficult to understand. Relatives often want to know if they are in some way "responsible" for his problems. With rare exception, the evidence suggests that relatives and friends do not cause psychiatric illness. Psychiatric illness develops from a complex combination of physical, biochemical, psychological, and social factors which make certain individuals susceptible to the development of psychiatric symptoms under certain conditions of stress. The specific mechanism is unknown; one widely held view is that difficulty in managing life's pressures may set in motion certain biochemical or physical changes in the body which, in turn, produce the symptoms of emotional illness. These physical changes and symptoms often persist after the pressure no longer exists. Indeed, it is often difficult to pinpoint the pressure. On the basis of this view, a person's relationships may be one factor, but it is unlikely that they can be considered the only factor.

Concerned relatives and friends may spend much time and emotional energy mulling over whether they are the "cause" of their loved one's problem. Such preoccupations are usually unproductive; in fact, the anxiety of relatives may be burdensome to the client. Relatives are better advised to look for ways to help. They may assume some of his responsibilities termporarily. It is often useful to discuss this with the therapist.

WHAT ROLE SHOULD RELATIVES AND FRIENDS PLAY IN ASSISTING THE CLIENT IN HIS TREATMENT?

The family and close friends of the client have an important role to play in psychiatric treatment, particularly in the earliest phases. The emotional support of his family and friends is a fundamental need of everyone, but especially of the person who is suicidal. Social isolation, rejection, and hostility are demoralizing and especially disturbing to the emotionally troubled. Insufficient understanding of psychiatric illness and the person's behavior often leads relatives and friends to act with too much firmness or pressure, which he may see as criticism or rejection.

An emotional crisis often signals that something is wrong in a family or between friends. A crisis exists when usual methods of coping with life's problems have failed. It can be a turning point, especially if the individual seeks professional help. Often it is discovered that a person has been suffering from an untreated chronic depression, which has not been recognized. A crisis can provide an opportunity for people to take a new and different look at themselves and their relationships with others. Frequently, more healthy and satisfying ways of living and relating to others can evolve from the changes which take place during and after a crisis.

Friends and relatives should not hesitate to seek the advice of one of the members of the center's staff to increase their understanding of their own uncertainty and anxiety. At times it is useful for relatives to enter psychotherapy, at the same time to resolve newly discovered difficulties of their own.

DO'S AND DON'TS

Friends and relatives can best help the client by supporting the treatment program that is recommended by the therapeutic team. While all specific questions should be referred to the therapist, there are a number of important "do's and don'ts" with which friends and relatives should be familiar.

Do's

1. *Do* remove all weapons and certain potentially dangerous medications from the environment. Recent studies suggest that suicide attempts are often beyond the individual's control and that they often occur impulsively. Insofar as the suicidal drive is often brief,

many suicides and suicide attempts can be prevented by not having the means available to those who in a moment of desperation might use them. Guns, in particular, should be removed from the home. Guns account for approximately 10,000 deaths by suicide in the United States each year. Poisons, barbiturates, and other potent medications also should be eliminated from the home. Barbiturates (sleeping medications) may so alter consciousness that the individual may be unaware of taking excessive amounts and may accidentally take a lethal overdose.

2. *Do* see that the person takes his medicine as prescribed, at the center. The administration of medication ("chemotherapy") is crucial for symptom relief and for return of full function. It takes some of the anti-depressant medicines several weeks to reach a therapeutic level in the bloodstream, so that immediate relief of symptoms is rarely possible. Knowing this can make waiting somewhat easier for the person. During the initial phase of chemotherapy, before any noticeable benefit can take place, the client may experience side effects such as drowsiness, constipation, and dry mouth. These usually disappear, or become tolerable, after a short period of time. Doubts about the usefulness of the medicine should be discussed with the doctor, who is the only person qualified to prescibe medication and evaluate its results. Relatives are not trained to do this and should refrain from making decisions in this matter. Doubts about the treatment in general should be discussed with the therapist, not the client. The expression of doubt may only serve to undermine confidence in the treatment and retard progress.

3. *Do* remember that most emergencies develop out of a failure to recognize the early warning signs of impending difficulty. It is important that relatives be aware of any changes in symptoms. If they notice an intensification of the following symptoms of emotional illness, they can be of great service to the individual and themselves urging the contacting of the therapist.

Sleep difficulties
Preoccupation with sad thoughts
Preoccupation with the disposition of possessions and arrangements
   of unfinished business
Poor appetite, or compulsive overeating
Loss of interest in the surroundings and in usual activities.
Loss of the ability to derive pleasure from the usual interests
Loss of sexual desire
Self-neglect
Crying and tearfulness
Lack of concentration and memory troubles
Hopelessness; suicidal thoughts or threats
Feelings of persecution
Unexplainable lifting of mood, euphoria, or excitement
Sudden calm in a previously agitated person

4. It is difficult to advise someone to get psychiatric treatment because of the stigma associated with psychiatric illness. The more one can focus on the symptoms about which the individual is complaining, especially socially acceptable symptoms like lack of energy, insomnia, and tension headaches, the easier it will be to make the recommendations to get help. The idea of intensive therapy to get to the psychological root of the problem is often difficult to accept. The idea of specific medicine for specific relief of specific symptoms, as in the treatment of physical illness, is more readily grasped and accepted. The person is usually not responsible for his symptoms and should not be made to feel so.

5. In the event of an emergency, try first to contact the Suicide Prevention Clinic in your area or nearest hospital emergency room, or one of the city emergency services which can be reached in many cities by dialing 911.

Don'ts

1. *Don't* undermine the person's confidence and faith in his

treatment by discussing with him doubts you might have about his treatment, or by recommending other clinics from which "miraculous" recoveries have been reported. While a second opinion can certainly help in the initial selection of physicians or clinics, discussion of his treatment with the person after he has started treatment may only serve to confuse and trouble him. Concerned relatives should discuss these issues first with the doctor, after securing the client's permission to do so.

2. Remember that psychiatric illness requires professional assessment and treatment, just as physical illnesses do. Don't become overinvolved in solving the person's problems. The hardest thing in the world for concerned relatives to do is to keep from offering friendly advice or trying out their own form of therapy. It is best not to push or prod the person to discuss his difficulties in an effort to "understand" the causes of his distress. This may only intensify his preoccupations. Discussions of this nature are best left to the therapist. When the client spontaneously discusses his distress, a calm, considerate attitude of listening can be very helpful. The person does not expect friends and relatives to have the answers. He just wants to know that they are interested and concerned. Just hearing him out when he wants to talk can be helpful.

3. *Don't* make demands on the person which might generate additional conflicts. Psychiatric patients often feel guilty and inadequate because their reduced energy prevents them from pursuing their usual activities. Retarded functioning is part of the illness and not within the person's control. Additional pressure only serves to heighten a sense of being a "burden." The time needed for recovery from psychiatric illnesses varies with each individual. Often it is some time before people feel up to resuming their usual life activities. During this recovery period, it is best for relatives to be supportive and sympathetic.

4. *Don't* assume the client's responsibilities. Excessive helpfulness can burden both him and the relative and generate much mutual

resentment. It is better to help the client to help himself than it is to do things for him that he himself can do, thereby undermining his self-confidence and slowing his recovery.

The Early Recognition and Treatment of Potentially Suicidal Persons

Ari Kiev

Practitioners in psychiatry and allied fields have focused much effort on developing techniques for the early recognition and treatment of psychiatric illness (commonly known as "mental disturbances" or "emotional disorders"). Certain basic principles have emerged from this work, knowledge of which may, help clients, their families, and others to cope more effectively and less fearfully with psychiatric illness.

DIFFICULTY IN RECOGNIZING PSYCHIATRIC ILLNESS

It is often difficult for people to recognize that they are in fact suffering from an abnormality of mood, thought, or behavior. The subjective experiences of normal life events may be so similar to the subjective experiences of emotional disorder that it is difficult for an individual to perceive any difference between the two. Some of the clients who visit therapists have been suffering from various symptoms for considerable periods of time, but the symptoms are so common in everyday life experience that they were not recognized as clinically treatable problems. Only when people begin to find it difficult to function do they look for help.

Even today, thousands of people associate psychiatric illness with the notion of someone going "stark raving mad" or having a "nervous breakdown" and being placed in a hospital (usually conceived of as a snakepit) in order to protect society from potential violence. This is a grossly unrealistic picture of psychiatric illness. Most psychiatric illnesses are temporary and self-limiting and do not become apparent even to the close, untrained onlooker except when he sees the person's social abilities and work performance decline.

The early symptoms of mental illness include very common experiences: difficulty in falling asleep, restless sleep, early morning awakening, loss of appetite or else compulsive overeating (with resultant weight gain), feeling blue or down in the dumps. The person—or his family—may blame noisy streets, a heavy dinner, fatigue, or work worries for such sleep difficulties, and pass them off as temporary and unimportant. Loss of appetite, sudden distaste for food, loss of weight, may go unnoticed or be explained away as the result of a change in diet, a desire to lose weight, or "gastric indigestion." The person's energy may drop so that simple, routine tasks become burdensome or even impossible; he may find it slowly and progressively more difficult to concentrate, lose interest in work and hobbies, find that his sexual drive has dropped off; he may become preoccupied with morbid thoughts, excessive worry, anxiety, fears, and pessimism coupled with guilt over being unable to perform or feel joy and other emotions. Sometimes the ill person will perceive the environment inaccurately and decide that co-workers or family and friends are either unsympathetic or actively hostile to him. He may find reasons to blame outside forces for the distress he feels. One of the difficulties in recognizing such a condition as a psychiatric illness is that the rationalizations sound quite plausible; he might indeed be under genuine stresses that would disturb anyone to some degree. It is precisely the degree, as a matter of fact, that determines the line between normal reaction to stress and the onset of a psychiatric condition.

Other individuals may find their thinking markedly disturbed, so that they cannot express ideas adequately or they misunderstand the ideas of others. They may then react by withdrawing from ordinary life experiences rather than suffer the strain caused by attempting to function.

To the extent that many of these symptoms can be temporary exaggerations of normal experiences, they often go unrecognized as the early signs of mental illness.

THE ONSET OF PSYCHIATRIC ILLNESS

Most persons, particularly in this society, tend to blame themselves or circumstances for these symptoms, consequently, they do not, or cannot, recognize them as early signs of psychiatric illness. Family, friends, colleagues, the ill person himself, are much more apt to feel that the symptoms are due to lack of will power, laziness, inadequacy, or personal failure. Less puritanical onlookers may blame the pressures of work, school, or family stresses. Loneliness, isolation, recent stressful experiences are even more acceptable explanations for symptoms; at least, less moral blame seems to be attached to them. But numerous studies have begun to suggest that symptoms first develop as a result of as yet unspecified physiological or biochemical changes in the nervous system. According to this view, interpersonal and psychological difficulties then *follow* on the development of the symptoms. Furthermore, old problems tend to be magnified and handled less well when someone is already emotionally ill. If the symptoms are successfully treated and relieved, however, the problems that seemed so overwhelming are reduced in magnitude, and the patient regains the ability to cope as well as he was able to before the onset of the illness.

SOME CAUSES LEADING PEOPLE TO ATTEMPT SUICIDE

Why do people attempt suicide? There can be a chain of reasons. A person experiencing the inner distress of emotional illness without recognizing that it *is* an illness that requires treatment—like pneumonia or Hong Kong flu—is apt to find it almost impossible to explain what is happening to him, or to explain his inability to perform. If he attempts to control the symptoms, or makes a greater effort and still fails, his sense of guilt and despair will heighten. Added to his own feelings of self-blame may be the judgments of others in his immediate environment who, not recognizing his real distress or the fact that his disturbances in sleep, appetite, energy, and drive are out of his control, may either criticize him or minimize his distress. They may insist that there is no real cause for his feelings and urge him to force himself to work and enjoy things. This kind of advice, well-meant as it may be, will only deepen the ill person's sense of helplessness and guilt. He may develop a pressing need to escape from both his own feelings and the additional guilt of being a burden to others. It is true that most people want to live; but not in a state of total distress. The tension that precedes the actual suicide attempt turns minutes into hours, days into unending nights, it so alters the person's capacity for rational judgment that he cannot even imagine that this tension state is really brief and self-limited.

EFFORTS TO GET RELIEF

The person suffering from these symptoms may try in many ways to get some relief. He may use tranquilizers—either prescribed or purchased over the counter—to reduce his anxiety and tension. He may get barbiturates or nonprescription sleeping pills to combat insomnia, and energy tonics for temporary and partial relief; but these stop-gap remedies can, in the end, be harmful if the underlying psychiatric illness is not recognized and treated. Some persons will search for new meanings to life or security through religions or philosophical movements; again, what for one person would be a rich, enlarging experience can, to the unrecognized psychiatric patient, be a potentially harmful experience, because the search has been motivated by an illness which will not be cured by these otherwise normal activities. When the search does not bring the longed-for relief, despair may deepen. Still others turn to excessive alcohol, or experiment with L.S.D. or other potent, dangerous, and sometimes addicting drugs which not only bring no relief but can lead to secondary complications more serious than the original illness.

THE ROLE OF SOCIAL FACTORS IN THE CAUSATION OF PSYCHIATRIC DISORDERS

The stresses of life associated with changes in the life cycle: adolescence, menopause and increasing age; the adjustment to new life situations such as marriage, death of a loved one, graduation from school, retirement, or the onset of a new career, may complicate psychiatric illnesses because of the extra demands they place on people. To the extent, however, that such experiences are used to rationalize the presence of symptoms, they may lead to the failure to recognize a treatable illness. For this reason, it is important to distinguish between natural life stresses and symptoms of emotional illness. Even if one "ought to feel depressed" because of a dreadful experience, adequate treatment can strengthen the individual's capacity to cope.

MENTAL ILLNESS AND EARLY LIFE EXPERIENCE

For a long time psychiatrists have thought that childhood experiences and the nature of family life were the exclusive causative factors in the development of psychiatric illness. As our knowledge has expanded we are now better able to distinguish among the contributions of past life experiences, heredity, chemistry and subsequent life experiences to the development of mental illnesses. As yet there is no true verdict as to how much these early life experiences contribute to the development of mental illnesses. They are important to the extent that they affect the individual's personality, adaptive skills, attitudes, and method of coping with illness. Parents too often feel unnecessarily responsible and guilty for the emotional illness of their children because of their obvious role in their children's development.

TREATMENT AVAILABLE FOR PSYCHIATRIC ILLNESS

Most often, treatment is flexible and relies on the advances of modern medicine, pharmacology, sociology, psychology, anthropology, public health, and other disciplines that contribute knowledge useful to the treatment of psychiatric illness. In the past decade, medicines have been discovered which help reduce and control specific target symptoms of psychiatric illness and make it possible to relieve much of the distress of these symptoms rapidly, economically, and in a relatively simple way. Antidepressant medication is useful for relieving insomnia, loss of appetite, loss of energy, depressed mood, and the marked emptiness and emotional inertia that patients often describe. Various major tranquilizers are useful for controlling patterns of repetitive and illogical thinking which are sometimes set in motion by emotional distress.

Medicine must be taken in adequate doses for a reasonable period of time. Some of the medicines require ten days to three weeks to reach an effective level in the body; to stop taking a medicine because it does not work immediately is a serious mistake. Side effects such as perspiration, dry mouth, constipation, sluggishness, dizziness, and blurring of vision may occur occasionally in the initial stages, but they are usually temporary. They are no cause for alarm, but they should be reported to the doctor who will adjust the dosage if he feels it is necessary. In no case should the patient stop taking the medicine without consulting his doctor, neither should he take medicines the doctor has not prescribed. Uncontrolled use of sleeping medications, tranquilizers, or stimulants such as dexedrine is potentially harmful and may complicate an unrecognized illness.

The magnitude and intensity of social and psychological problems and conflicts generally decrease as the patient's symptoms are relieved and he is restored to his normal emotional state. It is much easier to assess his problems at this stage. Difficulties on the job, at home, or in interpersonal relationships produce much guilt and may seem insoluble and overwhelming to the patient; nevertheless they may disappear, become completely manageable, or be reduced to just one problem area as the patient improves.

Still, efforts are made to alter any environmental circumstances that are clearly contributing to the person's illness. The frequency of visits to the therapist is based upon the extent of the person's distress and need for support during crisis periods. Sometimes it is desirable to see the patient every day if only for brief periods of time. At other times, it is enough to maintain telephone contact with the patient during crisis periods. For most patients a weekly visit over a period of one or two months will carry them through until their distress is enough relieved so that they are coping adequately again.

Personality changes do not come about, in the therapy session, but in real life situations, particularly when patients are able to experiment with new ways of being and behaving. This is particularly true for those individuals with chronic difficulties in adjustment and getting along. For this reason, treatment moves most rapidly when patients can focus on concrete problems in work, at home, or in interpersonal relationships, for these areas offer the greatest opportunity for trying out new ways of dealing with others, which can in turn lead to new attitudes and greater opportunities for self-realization.

The therapists act as guides in solving problems and try to assist the patient to help himself overcome those early learned habits and inhibitions which block him from pursuing his goals. While the professionals certainly do not have answers to all problems, there is good evidence that the effects of an individual's success in solving a previously insoluble problem are generalized to other areas of his life.

THE LENGTH OF EMOTIONAL ILLNESS

The vast majority of psychiatric illnesses, especially the depressive disorders, last some three to four months. Generally, it takes two to three weeks for medication to begin to work. The course of improvement may zig-zag, with good periods being followed sometimes by a temporary return of symptoms. However, the odds are that once the patient has begun to improve, overall progress will go uphill.

It takes considerably longer for attitudes and relationships to change. Once the patient discovers that each day is a new one affording him countless ordinary situations where he can try to realize himself and his potential by behaving in new ways, he can continue to progress on his own, periodically consulting with his therapist when and if new problems arise.

COMMUNITY RESOURCES AVAILABLE

There are a variety of community resources which are useful additions to treatment. These include not only specific rehabilitation and government supported training programs but a variety of recreational, cultural, social, religious, and educational activities which can help individuals to realize their potential through participation in the community.

DO'S AND DON'TS

Do's

1. The patient, his family and friends must recognize the importance of obtaining treatment for a diagnosed illness.
2. Report all symptoms, to your physician. Any change of mood, appetite, sleep pattern, drive, energy, concentration, and so forth.
3. Follow the doctor's advice.
4. Report all side-effects from medicine.
5. Keep a record of all medication taken. Should it be necessary to take other medicines, undergo surgery, or dentistry or be fitted for eye glasses, these records will ensure that undesirable mixtures will not be prescribed and the source of side effects will be understood.

Don'ts

1. *Don't* stop medicine unless specifically directed to do so, by the doctor.
2. *Don't* decrease or increase a medicine except at the doctor's direction.
3. *Don't* use any form of alcohol which may produce undesirable side-effects and/or complications and which may diminish the effectiveness of the medicine. Certain foods must be avoided when taking some types of anti-depressant medicine. It is important to follow the recommendations of the doctor who will advise you of this.
4. *Don't* take on unnecessary burdens while in treatment until it is apparent that you are definitely ready to do so.
5. *Don't* take responsibility for the illness. The patient's only responsibility is to recognize the illness, obtain competent professional help, and cooperate with the doctor or others on the medical

team. This is especially important for those who feel that they have caused their illness and are beyond help.

6. Avoid any major life change until you discuss this with the doctor, who may be better able to assess the decision objectively in relationship to the illness.

Subject Index

DATE DUE

MAY 23 '75
APR 9 1981
DEC 1 0 1981
OCT 7 1982
NOV 28 '75
FEB 1 6 76
DEC 9 1982
NOV 5 76
MAR 1 7 1983
MAR 03 77
APR 1 4 1983
MAY 26 77
OCT 6 1983
OCT 27 '77
NOV 24
3·2·84
AUG 21 78
DEC 6 1984
NOV 1 6 78
APR 5
DEC 2 7 1984
DEC 1 3 1979
JAN 3 1 1985
FEB 7 1980
MAR 2 1 1985
OCT 3 0 1980
APR 1 0 1986
FEB 5 1981

PRINTED IN U.S.A.

HIGHSMITH 45-220